Problems and Prospects
for
NUCLEAR WASTE DISPOSAL POLICY

Problems and Prospects
for
NUCLEAR WASTE DISPOSAL POLICY

Edited by
ERIC B. HERZIK
and
ALVIN H. MUSHKATEL

Prepared under the auspices of the Policy Studies Organization
Stuart S. Nagel, Publications Coordinator

Contributions in Political Science, Number 283

GREENWOOD PRESS
Westport, Connecticut • London

Library of Congress Cataloging-in-Publication Data

Problems and prospects for nuclear waste disposal policy / edited by
  Eric B. Herzik and Alvin H. Mushkatel.
      p.   cm. — (Contributions in political science, ISSN 0147–1066
  ; no. 283)
    Includes bibliographical references and index.
    ISBN 0–313–29058–X (alk. paper)
    1. Radioactive waste disposal—Government policy—United States.
  I. Herzik, Eric B. II. Mushkatel, Alvin H. III. Series.
  TD898.14.G68P76 1993
  363.72′8956′0973—dc20   93–4280

British Library Cataloguing in Publication Data is available.

Library of Congress Catalog Card Number: 93–4280
ISBN: 0–313–29058–X
ISSN: 0147–1066

First published in 1993

Greenwood Press, 88 Post Road West, Westport, CT 06881
An imprint of Greenwood Publishing Group, Inc.

Printed in the United States of America

The paper used in this book complies with the
Permanent Paper Standard issued by the National
Information Standards Organization (Z39.48–1984).

10 9 8 7 6 5 4 3 2 1

Contents

Illustrations

Preface

The nuclear age is just past fifty years old. What began as a terrible force of destruction for war was quickly transformed into a technological marvel for industrial and societal advancement. With the promise of electricity too cheap to meter and applications for industry and medicine, nuclear power proliferated throughout the 1950s through the 1970s.

One of the greatest promises of nuclear energy was its ability to seemingly deliver so much power with so little disruption to the environment. Gone were the smokestacks of coal-generated power plants and even the disruption to the landscape caused by hydro-electric power stations. In the rush to promote nuclear power, little thought was given to nuclear waste. There was a general faith that technical solutions could easily deal with any problems posed by nuclear waste.

Nuclear power has traveled a far rockier road since the mid-1970s. Public concerns have all but ground the expansion of nuclear power to a stop. A primary issue of public concern is the recognition that no long-term policy solutions exist for the disposal of nuclear wastes. With deadly contamination from such wastes lasting as long as 10,000 years, the early faith in technological solutions has been lost. It is now recognized that technology is just one of many factors driving the development of nuclear waste disposal policies.

This book examines the dynamics of nuclear waste disposal policy. We have organized the book to address a wide range of issues found in the nuclear waste disposal policy debate—whether these wastes be high-level or low-level. Chapters 1 through 3 are broad cuts at the policymaking environment. Chapters 4 through 8 cover more specific management and policy concerns. The concluding two chapters are case studies of policy development and implementation. The overall goal is to discuss both the problems policymakers face in fashioning nuclear waste disposal policies and to offer some insights as to the prospects for improved policy development.

As with most scholarly efforts, this book is the product of a large array of individuals. The basic work was provided by the chapter authors. Stuart Nagel played his usual key role in providing general assistance and support. The expertise of David Pijawka was a great asset on which we could draw. The Department of Political Science at the University of Nevada provided material support. Finally, we owe considerable thanks to Larissa Alonso, who as much as anyone helped edit and get the manuscript ready for publication.

Problems and Prospects
for
NUCLEAR WASTE DISPOSAL POLICY

1

When Rationality and Good Science Are Not Enough: Science, Politics, and the Policy Process

ERIC B. HERZIK *and* E. ROBERT STATHAM

The development of nuclear waste policies in the United States has been anything but consensual and is often stalemated. In large part this reflects the neglect given the back end of the fuel cycle as the use of nuclear energy quickly expanded in the 1950s through the 1970s (Wilson, 1979; Herzik, 1993). At a time when the nuclear industry enjoyed a nearly total hegemony over the policy process (Baumgartner and Jones, 1991; Thurber, 1991) waste disposal policies were not developed. Now, with the nuclear industry challenged on multiple fronts, every waste policy initiative becomes an arduous political struggle.

The history of the breakdown of the nuclear industry's control over the policymaking process has been the subject of several studies (Carter, 1987; Jacob, 1990; Baumgartner and Jones, 1991). The preponderance of blame for this breakdown has generally fallen on the weak management and control record of various government regulatory and policymaking bodies, and the lack of input granted diverse entities in the fashioning and oversight of nuclear policy development (Kraft, 1992; Herzik, 1993). Despite these criticisms nuclear waste remains a problem that must be addressed. At present there are a wide range of nuclear wastes in temporary storage. By the year 2000, the volume of various wastes is estimated to include more than 88,000 tons of high-level wastes and 3.5 million tons of low-level wastes (U.S. GAO, 1981). Indeed, it often seems as if the existence of these wastes and their current storage safety and health risks are lost in political battles among state and local governments, environmental groups, the nuclear industry, and federal regulatory agencies.

The jockeying for political victories in the waste policy process— whether these victories be the successful siting of a facility or the blockage of a site—often reflects an underlying lack of communication among the actors involved in the process (Clary, 1992). For the most part, the federal regulatory agencies and nuclear industry view the process as involving technical solutions relying on good science ultimately translated into rational policy solutions. In contrast, local opposition groups and state governments are generally more attuned to issues of equity, public acceptability, and more nebulous value choices in policymaking.

This chapter argues that the elements of equity, acceptability, and values have come to dominate the nuclear waste policymaking process. These elements are not conducive to resolution through a traditional, and fairly limited, rational policymaking process, and until federal decisionmakers and the nuclear industry recognize the limits of the rational policy and good science approach, nuclear waste disposal policy will continue to be stalemated. We further conclude that recognition of the priority of politics in nuclear waste policymaking may ultimately necessitate more authoritarian decisionmaking in selecting waste disposal sites, although such political solutions should be approached with extreme caution and properly safeguard public input.

We begin with a discussion of the structure of rational policymaking that underlies the federal agency and industry approach to nuclear waste policy development. We then discuss how a naive model of "good science" combines with the rational policy approach. Problems with that approach are identified. We then discuss the lack of commensurability between policy approaches among various actors in the process and note that decisionmaking may ultimately rest not on consensus but on a more majoritarian allocation of values.

METHODISM, RATIONALISM, AND POLICY ANALYSIS

U.S. public policy analysis has been primarily directed and ordered by a profound emphasis on rationality. Indeed, a recent assessment of the policy field concluded that methodological rigor and rationality are closely linked to professional legitimacy. What is required is "empirical research which aspires to be rigorous, or will be updated in the future with more rigor—especially if previous research about a subject was not so rigorous" (Wall, 1984:406).

Why policy analysis has been animated by a quest for rationality and methodological rigor can be explained in part by the generally desired purpose of the activity itself: "There is a modest consensus that social research can and should be relevant to immediate policy concerns" (Paris and Reynolds, 1983:1). Policy concerns, which are by definition public, are thus proposals for government action. The proposals are, at least in a rational policy approach, then assessed using the best methodological tools available and fashioned into practical policy responses.

Harold Lasswell, one of the patriarchs of U.S. policy analysis, summarizes the relationship among methodological rigor, rationality, and practicality in defining the purpose of policy analysis.

> We provisionally define the policy sciences as concerned with knowledge of and in the decision process. As a professional man, the policy scientist is concerned with mastering the skills appropriate to enlightened decision-making in the context of public and civic order. As a professional man who shares the scientist's disciplined concern for the empirical, he is searching for an optimum synthesis of the diverse skills that contribute to a dependable theory and practice of problem solving in the public interest. (1971:4)

The purpose of policy analysis is matched to a distinct process. While a variety of more or less elaborate rational policy models exist, the basic elements of the approach are outlined by Deborah Stone (1988:5):

1. Identify objectives.
2. Identify alternative courses of action for achieving objectives.
3. Predict and evaluate possible consequences of each alternative.
4. Select the alternative that maximizes the attainment of objectives.

The manner of thought prescribed by this model is technical, procedural, and calculative. Methodical thinking is preferred since it offers likelihood of improved efficiency and successful results based on workable techniques that prove to be both regular and predictable in operation (Wolin, 1969).

GOOD SCIENCE AND RATIONAL POLICYMAKING

The work of Lasswell and the whole genre of rational policy analysis rests on two fundamental points: (1) that knowledge is empirically derived from the environment, and (2) that knowledge is and ought to be socially useful. At this point the rational policy model and modern scientific thought coalesce. Indeed, Lasswell acknowledges in the quote above the linkage between the professional policy analyst and the scientist in the search for dependable theory based on empirical methods. In following a rational course of analysis both the policy analyst and the natural scientist are ultimately led to the uncovering of facts.

The process described parallels Ludwig Wittgenstein's delineation of a "criterion of meaningfulness." In distinguishing science from philosophy, Wittgenstein notes:

> The totality of true propositions is the total natural science. . . . This means that the propositions which belong to science are those deducible from true observation statements; they are those propositions which can be verified by true observation statements. Could we know all true observation statements, we would also know all that may be asserted by natural science. (1961:49)

Once the facts are in place, determination of a scientific conclusion (or a practical policy response) becomes largely a *fait accompli*.

The pursuit of "facts" in science leads to a situation where scientists rarely examine the questions they may address, but focuses instead on "concrete problem solutions that the profession has come to accept as paradigms" (Kuhn, 1977:166). It also places a high premium on particular kinds of knowledge. Information that does not match the prevailing code of scientific method is downgraded (Fleming, 1992). The ultimate goal is "objectivism" or "the basic conviction that there is or must be some permanent, ahistorical matrix or framework to which we can ultimately appeal in determining the nature of rationality, knowledge, truth, reality, goodness or rightness" (Bernstein, 1983:8).

A number of analysts have both directly and indirectly assessed the prevalence of the code of objective science in various federal agencies dealing with nuclear regulatory and environmental issues (Thurber, 1991; Herzik, 1993; Bupp and Derian, 1981; Moody, 1990; Meier et al., 1990; Bartlett, 1991). For some (Moody, 1990; Meier et al., 1990) there is an implicit faith that better understanding of science by the public will lead to acceptance of the basically sound science-based decisions of the agencies charged with overseeing technical issues such as nuclear waste disposal. For others (Bupp and Derian, 1981; and to a lesser extent Herzik, 1993) the insularity of science has led to a general failure of nuclear energy policies. In reviewing these and other historical assessments (see in particular Carter, 1987), we conclude that the development of nuclear policies in the United States has been dominated by agencies with a distinctive scientific bias—a bias that reflects the rational policy/good science paradigm as discussed briefly above.

THE PROBLEMS OF RATIONALITY AND GOOD SCIENCE

Modern scientific thought and rational policy models are grounded in a belief in the possibility of vast improvement in the human condition—here and now. This grounding requires the conscious depreciation of certain kinds of thought (such as contemplation of forms or philosophical ideals) and entails placing primary emphasis upon method; upon how one thinks as opposed to what one thinks about (Kress, 1979). It is not our intent to completely eschew or disparage the theoretical underpinnings or the potential benefits of this approach. However, the approach contains a variety of shortcomings which, if not addressed, may lead to an ultimate frustration of policy development. Theoretical, scientific, and political challenges all give reason to pause and reconsider the use of an unrestrained rational-scientific approach to decisionmaking. We will briefly consider a series of these challenges and their implications for nuclear waste policy development.

Theoretical Challenges

There is a long history in the philosophy of science literature that challenges the basic thrusts of the rational science and policy models. Perhaps the best known is the work of Karl Popper. Popper criticizes most scientific thinking as being naively positivistic. His goal is to show that induction and verification, core elements of the most basic scientific thinking, are illusory; they are predicated on a false confidence in the predictability of the future and the objectivity of empirical observation (1962).

Popper argues against the ability of science to adequately predict the future. He refers to knowledge based on empirical observation as being "tentative" and claims that our confidence that the future will be like the past is not a scientific certitude but an undemonstrable faith. While scientific experiment and empirical observation seemingly buttress the faith in predictive utility, he notes the circularity of the scientific sequence. Specifically, the very manner in which we verify the future is to show what path past cases have followed. Yet this is the very thing that science hopes to show, that the future follows the past.

Popper's critique attacks the very method by which science unfolds as being little more than self-fulfilling prophecy. He begins by noting that science generally fails to consider the context of empirical observation. Observation, the critical first step in developing scientific hypotheses, takes place in response to a predetermined problem that directs the researcher toward some data while ignoring other data. In essence, the knowledge gained from observation is dependent on the knowledge we already possess.

This critique sets in motion the rejection of the fact/value distinction that is central to the objectivism of rational science and policy models. The critique is extended by Richard Bernstein (1983), who claims that the search for objectivism is rooted in a Cartesian anxiety that seeks stability in a fixed foundation of facts on which knowledge must rest. However, such stability comes at a cost: that of a scientific method that is doomed to simply verify itself by casting out ideas and data that do not conform to conventional paradigms (Kuhn, 1970).

There are practical implications for nuclear waste policymaking in the critiques of Popper and other philosophers of science. In analyzing nuclear waste issues, the Department of Energy (DOE) and the nuclear industry regularly exhort their use of the best minds and methods of the scientific community. However, the uncertainty associated with analysis of nuclear wastes leads the scientific community away from a broad-based assessment of the problem and into naive positivism (Fleming, 1992). Following from the above critique, this leads to little more than existing science verifying future science. In so doing, more imaginative analysis and explicitly value-oriented research are relegated to "emotive status, making them unamenable to rational discourse" (ibid.:119). As discussed more fully below, such exclusions can undermine the credibility of science and the perceived legitimacy of policy decisionmaking.

Scientific Challenges

While the underlying philosophy of rational science and policy models can lead to questions of legitimacy in the grander process of scientific discovery, the specific application of science with regard to nuclear waste raises a series of scientific doubts about existing policy choices. In attempting to assess the safety of various nuclear disposal technologies, policymakers rely largely on empirical observation. However, the nuclear waste policy time frame—often stretched to cover disposal for 10,000 years—defies the ability of empirical science to deliver answers with absolute certainty. The very "facts" rational science and policy models strive for are often in dispute.

In part such disputes are a traditional aspect of science. Conflicting theories and hypotheses should be held up to scrutiny and modified as needed. However, this process of science-as-a-separate-end-unto-itself is problematic when matched with the process of public policy decisionmaking. As Diane Meier and her colleagues observe:

> In areas where new ideas and methods are being considered, the uncertainty about projected results may generate debate among scientists. While this debate may be a healthy element of the scientific process, it may have three negative effects on the public's views of scientists. First, the problems involved in projecting the consequences of science and technology are emphasized. Second, science loses its aura of objectivity and rationality when there are arguments about interpretation of findings. Third, the integrity of scientists themselves becomes an issue; the public seems to view debates among experts as evidence that scientific findings are "rigged" to justify particular positions. (1990:221)

In response to shortcomings in empirically assessing the elements of nuclear waste disposal technologies, policymakers and scientists are often forced to resort to simulation models and expert judgments. In so doing, objectivism is replaced by surrogate judgments of the individual modelers and experts. This further extends the critique of the philosophers of science that empirical observation is biased by past conventions. As Patricia Fleming concludes, "When faced with the conflict of interpretations and clamour of voices [about nuclear wastes] . . . we are fooling ourselves by thinking that scientific expert opinion is the Archimedean point of stability in this world of uncertainty" (1992:119).

Political Challenges

With scientific certainty undermined, there is fertile ground for political manipulation of the policy and scientific process. Indeed, the severest challenges to nuclear waste policy development have come in the form of political and social concerns questioning the science underlying the analysis of nuclear waste policy.

Perhaps the foremost political challenge concerns the issue of public trust in the safety of nuclear waste repositories. The public's general confidence in institutions has declined markedly over the past three decades (Lipset and Schneider, 1983; Meier et al., 1990). Trust in DOE and the nuclear industry appears to fall below most other governmental and business institutions (Pijawka and Mushkatel, 1992). In large part this reflects the special concern the public associates with nuclear projects. It may also be linked to the generally poor management and communication history of the various government entities charged with regulating U.S. nuclear development (Herzik, 1993; Herzik and Mushkatel, 1992).

The issue of trust presents a particularly puzzling problem for scientists and rational policymakers. When faced with decreasing trust in science and the institutions associated with scientific analysis, scientists and rational policymakers attempt to do better science. Redundancy in both study methodology and project design becomes exaggerated. Evidence is marshaled to show that the risk probabilities realistically faced by the public are exceedingly low. Public information and education campaigns become more salient. Yet, distrust persists and seems little moved by the best efforts of scientists attempting to do better science.

For the scientist and rational policymaker the public's lack of trust is generally deemed irrational. In terms of statistical probabilities of risk, it is hard not to conclude there is an irrational fear of nuclear waste (and nuclear elements generally). Some theorists have produced post-hoc defenses that make the public's fears seemingly more rational (Freudenberg, 1987; Slovic et al., 1991). For these authors, because nuclear elements contain the potential, no matter how small, for catastrophic results, and because the public has no control over nuclear catastrophe entering their lives, exaggerated public fears take on a certain rationality. These defenses are hardly convincing given the whole host of other potentially catastrophic items that might affect public health and over which the individual has seemingly little control. Rather, it appears that the public has been scared by nuclear-related issues and it is now hard to "unscare" them (Kasperson, 1991).

The public's fear of nuclear-related items results in part from the management secrecy and aloofness of science maintained by the agencies of government charged with initially overseeing nuclear development (Herzik, 1993). Thus, government agencies and nuclear scientists are paying for past sins. However, it would be naive to think that opponents of nuclear development and waste policies don't capitalize on the public's fears. For example, statements by groups opposed to the high-level nuclear waste repository in Nevada (including state officials) concerning nuclear plants exploding like atomic bombs and cities becoming ghost towns from nuclear waste spills are potent images for Nevadans. The questioning of scientific findings, as noted above, further muddies the issue environment and detracts from rational consideration of scientific and policy issues.[1]

Again, the response of the scientific community is to fall back on good science. Issues are given to referees such as the National Academy of Sciences or special technical committees. The effect for the public is generally not to be swayed by the process of science, but to have fears heightened by the seemingly disputable and conflicting facts.

MAKING POLICY WITH UNCERTAINTY

The challenges to rational science and policymaking noted above are certainly not exhaustive. Rather, they demonstrate that rational science and policymaking is an incomplete approach for developing nuclear waste policy. This is not meant to imply that good science and rational policymaking should be eschewed. What must be sought is a blending of the rationality of science with broader societal values and political decisionmaking processes.

For a variety of reasons noted above and by others, society will never be absolutely certain that any nuclear waste disposal policy will be risk free. Indeed, this standard of absolute safety is a false goal. Rather, society should strive for the *safest acceptable* policy option. We emphasize the two words above as they contain relative judgments. Safety is relative to various associated risk probabilities. At one level, calculating the various risk probabilities makes this criterion most amenable to the processes of good science. However, safety will only take on meaning by the level of risk acceptable to the public.

Public acceptance of a project is, as our brief discussion of trust above illustrates, far from being a strictly rational calculus or scientific determination. It is not totally irrational, but instead is marked by a value calculus in face of uncertainty. When public concern about risk increases, the public demands a greater role in policy decisionmaking (Meier et al., 1990). The input of experts, while included, may be devalued in the pursuit of other value goals. There is a certain irony in a public calculation that downplays scientific input, as science and rational policymaking often rejects the value goals the public seeks to weigh in their policy deliberations.

At base the policy model of the general public in approaching nuclear waste issues appears to be far more inclusive than that of a good science or rational policy model. The two decisionmaking approaches are in many ways incommensurate, but are not totally irreconcilable. As Fleming argues, there is the opportunity for all sides to communicate on the issue. Such communication should not ignore standards in the scientific sense, "but it denies that they are ahistorical" (1992:118).

NUCLEAR WASTE POLICIES AS POLITICAL CHOICES

Nuclear waste policies embody a wide range of inputs covering basic technical information (e.g., ground water diffusion rates through differing rock media) and societal values such as the intergenerational consequences of long-term waste storage. This range of inputs clearly places nuclear waste policy decisionmaking into the political arena, for it is most likely in the political arena that such widely divergent inputs can be reconciled.

Recognizing the primacy of politics in nuclear waste policy development should alter the policymaking process. In contrast with many authors (Kraft, 1992; Clary, 1992; Slovic et al., 1991) we believe that recognition of the more political nature of nuclear waste policy development lessens the need for consensus. Indeed, true, or even partial, consensus is an impossibility given the widely divergent goals of the actors involved in nuclear waste policy decisionmaking.

Forsaking the false promise of consensus should not be viewed as a major flaw in the political approach to policy development. Rather, it reflects the nature of nearly all policy decisionmaking in the U.S. system, where consensus is not the norm. Consensus rarely is found except in some basic agreement that a problem exists and policy action may be desirable. These specific policy actions become the subject of oftentimes intense debate. Policy decisions are generally reached not by consensus but by majoritarian deliberation. Such is the case for nearly every environmental policy developed in this country, whether the topic be hazardous waste, air pollution, energy consumption, or transportation. Nuclear waste follows a similar pattern. There is consensus that wastes should be contained using the best mix of engineering, natural, and administrative controls. However, just what specifically constitutes the best mix is subject to intense disagreement.

Critics will quickly note that the political approach will yield a less than optimal solution. Indeed, the very environmental policies noted above can be offered as proof of the failure of political decisionmaking to produce optimal outcomes. Such criticism is myopic and ultimately suffers the same flaws that infect the rational scientific model. In arguing that optimality may not be achieved, we simply note that the seemingly nonoptimal solution reflects the prior value orientations of the critics: *qua*, not optimal by whose standard? This, ironically, returns us to the criticism of rational science's inability to recognize the context of empirical observation. Optimality is a false goal, defined more by one's own biases and method. The political model will lead to a "satisficing" of interests (Simon, 1945), which approximates optimality, or the *best acceptable* solution, in a pluralistic society.

An additional criticism is that nuclear wastes are unique due to their potentially catastrophic outcomes. Yet the potential for catastrophe presented by long-term air pollution or mishandled hazardous materials is no less significant and may be, in a statistical sense, more likely to occur. (Other potentially catastrophic occurrences can also be found in policy arenas other than the environment, such as military or transportation policy.) The political model allows for the direct consideration of values such as public trust and social equity, but these values cannot be considered in isolation or in response to some predetermined uniqueness of the policy item to be considered. If critics of scientific insularity desire an expanded policy environment driven by public concerns, they must also bear the consequences when the public domain makes a decision contrary to their policy bias.

Relying on political determination is hardly a novel approach in policy decisionmaking. Indeed, it is the norm for U.S. policymaking, and nuclear wastes fit easily into a normal pattern of policymaking. Ironically, political decisionmaking is often castigated by all sides in the nuclear waste policy debate. For the rational science followers, politics is seen as an irrational jumble that will lead to nonoptimal solutions. For many groups opposed to nuclear waste facilities, politics is seen as also producing nonoptimal solutions in service of powerful vested interests. As noted, both sides suffer from an illusion of optimality that is defined largely by their own biases. Both also fail to place nuclear waste policymaking into the process by which U.S. public policy decisions are ultimately made: more-or-less publicly sanctioned deliberations by political entities vested with the power to authoritatively allocate values.

CONCLUSION

To some, an argument relying on a pluralistic political process will never be satisfactory. We maintain that to pursue any other goal rejects the basic nature of the U.S. policymaking process and ultimately removes the public from considering a full range of factors in fashioning nuclear waste policies. Such rejection will only continue policy stalemate as an elusive consensus fails to emerge.

Policy planners should not be shy in relying on the political process and a search for majoritarian rather than consensual choices. However, the process must be open to all sorts of inputs, whether they be water diffusion models from university scientists or the views of native peoples concerning the sacredness of the land. The system must also not be held hostage by any particular group, whether these groups be from the nuclear industry or local environmental activists. Following E. E. Schattschneider (1960), it is only by expanding the scope of conflict and bringing the full range of public interests into the waste policy decisionmaking process that legitimate policies will be developed. The end result may be that particular local or state interests will be forced to accept policies they do not prefer. However, such policy choice is hardly unique and is ultimately the only way in which not-in-my-backyard (NIMBY) attitudes and other parochial roadblocks in the nuclear waste policy development process may be overcome.

NOTE

1. A classic example of the political use of science is found in the jockeying between DOE and the state of Nevada over the so-called Symanski Report. Jerry Symanski, a scientist for DOE, produced a study theorizing that groundwater at the proposed Yucca Mountain nuclear waste site actually flowed upward in dramatic surges. His report was based on a single cross-section of rock sample. DOE held the report pending further study. Nevada's Nuclear Waste Project Office (NWPO) immediately released the report's findings and claimed that DOE was silencing potentially damaging scientific evidence. Symanski's report was subsequently reviewed by the National Academy of Sciences (NAS) and unanimously rejected on both theoretical grounds and empirical findings from more extensive rock study samples. However, the NWPO and various antidump groups in Nevada still report the Symanski findings and some have even claimed that the NAS was "bought off" by DOE.

REFERENCES

Bartlett, Robert V. 1991. The Significance of the "New Institutionalism" for Research on Environmental Politics and Policy. Paper presented at the Workshop on Research in Environmental Politics and Policy, American Political Science Association Annual Meeting, Washington, DC, August 28.

Baumgartner, Frank and Bryan Jones. 1991. Agenda Dynamics and Policy Subsystems. *Journal of Politics*, 53, 4:1044–1076.

Bernstein, Richard J. 1983. *Beyond Objectivism and Relativism*. Philadelphia: University of Pennsylvania Press.

Bupp, Irvin and Jean-Claude Derian. 1981. *The Failed Promise of Nuclear Power*. New York: Harper & Row.

Carter, Luther. 1987. *Nuclear Imperatives and Public Trust: Dealing with Radioactive Waste*. Washington, DC: Resources for the Future.

Clary, Bruce. 1992. The Enactment of the Nuclear Waste Policy Act of 1982. *Policy Studies Review*, 10, 4:90–102.

Fleming, Patricia. 1992. Expert Judgment and High-Level Nuclear Waste Management. *Policy Studies Review*, 10, 4:114–126.

Freudenberg, William R. 1987. Rationality and Irrationality in Estimating the Risks of Nuclear Waste Disposal. Paper presented at Waste Management '87, Tucson, Arizona.

Herzik, Eric B. 1993. State Government Roles in Nuclear Waste Disposal Policy. In Fred
    Meyer and Ralph Baker, eds. *State Policy Problems*. Chicago: Nelson-Hall
    (forthcoming).
Herzik, Eric B. and Alvin Mushkatel. 1992. Intergovernmental Complexity in Nuclear
    Waste Disposal Policy. *Policy Studies Review*, 10, 4:139–151.
Jacob, Gerald. 1990. *Site Unseen: The Politics of Siting a Nuclear Waste Repository*.
    Pittsburgh: University of Pittsburgh Press.
Kasperson, Roger E. 1991. Social Realities in High-Level Radioactive Waste Manage-
    ment. In *Proceedings of the International High-Level Radioactive Waste Manage-
    ment Conference*. New York: American Society of Civil Engineers.
Kraft, Michael. 1992. Public Responses to High-Level Nuclear Waste Disposal. *Policy
    Studies Review*, 10, 4:152–166.
Kress, Paul. 1979. Against Epistemology: Apostate Musings. *Journal of Politics*, 41, 2:
    526–542.
Kuhn, Thomas. 1970. *The Structure of Scientific Revolution*, 2nd ed. Chicago: University
    of Chicago Press.
———. 1977. *The Essential Tension*. Chicago: University of Chicago Press.
Lasswell, Harold D. 1971. *A Pre-View of Policy Sciences*. New York: Elsevier.
Lipset, Seymour M. and William Schneider. 1983. *The Confidence Gap*. Baltimore: Johns
    Hopkins Press.
Meier, Diane, Wilma C. Probst and Phillip Niedzielski-Eichner. 1990. Public Involve-
    ment: Keystone to Public Confidence in the Civilian Radioactive Waste Manage-
    ment Program. In *High Level Radioactive Waste Management*, vol. 1. La Grange
    Park, IL: American Nuclear Society.
Moody, Helen. 1990. Where's the Rabbit? Translating Science and Technology. In *High
    Level Radioactive Waste Management*, vol. 1. La Grange Park, IL: American
    Nuclear Society.
Paris, David C. and James F. Reynolds. 1983. *The Logic of Policy Inquiry*. New York:
    Longman.
Pijawka, K. David and Alvin K. Mushkatel. 1992. Public Opposition to the Siting of the
    High-Level Nuclear Waste Repository. *Policy Studies Review*, 10, 4:180–194.
Popper, Karl. 1962. *Conjectures and Refutations*. New York: Basic Books.
Schattschneider, E. E. 1960. *The Semisovereign People*. New York: Holt, Rinehart,
    Winston.
Simon, Herbert. 1945. *Administrative Behavior*. New York: Macmillan.
Slovic, Paul, Mark Layman and James H. Flynn. 1991. Risk Perception, Trust, and
    Nuclear Waste. *Environment*, 33, 3:6–11, 26–28.
Stone, Deborah A. 1988. *Policy Paradox and Political Reason*. Boston: Scott, Foresman
    & Co.
Thurber, James. 1991. Congressional Oversight of High-Level Nuclear Waste Disposal
    Policy. Paper delivered to the Annual Meeting of the American Political Science
    Association, Washington, DC, August 31–September 2.
U.S. General Accounting Office. 1981. Coal and Nuclear Wastes: Both Potential Con-
    tributors to Environmental and Health Problems. Report no. EMD–81–132 (Sep-
    tember 21).

Wall, Phillip C. 1984. Recent Trends in Public Policy Analysis. *Polity*, 17, 2:404–415
Wilson, Carroll L. 1979. Nuclear Energy: What Went Wrong. *Bulletin of Atomic Scientists*, 36, 6:13–18.
Wittgenstein, Ludwig. 1961. *Tractatus Logico-Philosophicus*. London: Routledge & Kegan Paul.
Wolin, Sheldon S. 1969. Political Theory as a Vocation. *American Political Science Review*, 63, 4:1062–1065.

2

Beyond Yucca Mountain and Environmental Gridlock: An Alternative Future for Nuclear Waste Policy

BRUCE B. CLARY

In recent years, the concept of environmental gridlock has drawn much attention. The problem is evident at all levels of government. In the face of significant environmental problems, especially those which generate strong public concern about risks, government is unable to act (Kraft, 1990).

The gridlock is most evident for toxic and hazardous waste disposal, including nuclear waste. The dynamics of the impasse are well known (O'Hare et al., 1983). Society has the responsibility to dispose of the wastes in as safe a manner as possible. Despite the widespread social benefits resulting from responsible disposal, there is also the potential for highly concentrated costs. If the waste material "leaks" into the surrounding environment, the population in the facility's air or watershed can be at substantial risk.

In one siting effort after another, proponents are unable to convince those individuals who perceive themselves to be at risk that the facility is safe. A waste disposal facility needs to be sited, but citizens stand in implacable opposition. Compromise solutions elude decisionmakers. The result is a stalemate with the issue remaining unresolved, often for years on end (Andrews and Pierson, 1985).

The high-level nuclear waste issue may be the most prominent of these gridlocks. It has a forty-year history and since the 1970s the federal government and the states have been in perpetual conflict over how and where to site a facility (Carter, 1987). However, the congressional decision in 1987 to restrict further search to one location, Yucca Mountain, Nevada, may represent one way to surmount this gridlock. Congress took this action in December 1987 as an amendment to the Nuclear Waste Policy Act of

1982 (NWPA). The title of Part E of the amendment was "Redirection of the Nuclear Waste Program." It required the U.S. Department of Energy (DOE) to start a phase-out of all site-specific activities at candidate locations. The only exception was Yucca Mountain in the state of Nevada. All future analysis was restricted to that site.

Congress substituted a political decision for a process based upon public participation and science in choosing a final site. Previous efforts generated widespread citizen resistance and many scientific criticisms of the siting methodology. By focusing on one site, Congress may have found a way around this controversy. Instead of bargaining with many different states where potential sites were located, the federal government only had to deal with Nevada. The more complex scientific question of which site is best was replaced by a simpler one: does the Yucca Mountain site meet the criteria for the acceptable location of a repository?

This chapter focuses on the congressional decision to restrict further search to one location. Only time will tell whether Yucca Mountain has set a precedent in how to deal with the gridlock of high-level nuclear waste and, possibly, other policy areas where similar stalemates exist. The decision is representative of a growing sentiment that government must take an authoritative role in settlement of the not-in-my-backyard (NIMBY) impasse. Certain states (Florida, New York, and New Jersey) have created agencies which have the power to impose siting decisions upon local communities (Matheny and Williams, 1985; Heiman, 1990). Some argue that citizen participation in decisionmaking should be substantially curtailed, including denial of the right to sue and vote on a site (Delogu, 1990:214). Consequently, the Yucca Mountain decision is not only central in understanding high-level nuclear waste policy development, but also has relevance for other NIMBY gridlocks (Malone, 1991).

This chapter explores how the 1987 amendments might have been written to reflect what was learned from the implementation experience of the 1982 act. The purpose is to suggest alternatives to the use of political power as a sole solution to the high-level nuclear waste gridlock and similar controversies that may arise now and in the future. A model of institutional policy analysis, developed by William Gormley in 1987, forms the basis of the analysis. It is outlined below along with its specific application to the case study.

CONCEPTUAL FRAMEWORK

The Yucca Mountain decision embodied in the 1987 Nuclear Waste Policy Act Amendments is a procedural one. It changed the basic process of siting a nuclear waste repository. To draw from Gormley, Yucca Mountain is a study in "governance redesign." Congress did more than simply amend the NWPA when it enacted the section on "redirection of the nuclear waste program." It set an important institutional precedent for handling of the NIMBY issue. While a critical decision in the evolution of nuclear waste policy, it has significant implications beyond this policy arena. Will Congress or other legislative bodies, when faced with similar public outcries in the future, resort to the authoritative exercise of power which Yucca Mountain represents? Gormley's approach suggests three ways to approach the issue.

Remedies Versus Opportunities

In most cases of policy reform, the dominant concern in legislatures and among policy analysts is how to remedy problems, most often using previously tried approaches. Less emphasis is given to the search for new alternatives which might offer more promise, but which pose political and other kinds of uncertainty. This orientation should not be unexpected given the prominence of incrementalism in Congress and other governmental institutions.

In analyzing the Yucca Mountain decision, we need to ask what other institutional or procedural directions could have been taken. The actual decision to restrict the search to a Nevada site was only one of several options. What would the amendments to the 1982 act have looked like if Congress had not been so reactive? In the rush to decision, Congress ignored alternatives which might have placed nuclear waste policy on firmer ground, scientifically and politically. One of this chapter's purposes is to analyze these options as well as to explore the implications of the Yucca Mountain decision.

Formal Versus Informal Reforms

Organizational change in government is often the result of formal decisions to adopt new procedures or reorganize existing agencies. However, change can occur in informal ways as well. An illustration is an agreement between agencies which can accomplish the same goals as legislation requiring formal, joint action. Gormley states that informal arrangements have distinct advantages. If they do not work out, agencies can try something else without the requirement of legislative approval, often a drawn-out and conflictual process.

One value of informal reform is that it often results from policy learning. Like individuals, organizations grow and adapt through the acquisition of information and its application to particular situations, learning what works and what does not. For example, Richard Barke (1985) applies policy learning theory to the Resource Conservation and Recovery Act of 1976 in showing how Congress responded effectively to inadequacies in the legislation, especially to problems in Environmental Protection Agency (EPA) implementation of it. In particular, Congress used new scientific knowledge about the hazardous waste problem in the evaluation of policy alternatives. More often, however, science has a limited impact upon policy due to the slowness in which changes in problem definition occur.

Congress, in its reconsideration of the 1982 legislation, acted in a manner that reflected little about what could be learned from past experiences with the scientific dimensions of siting. Its behavior reflected the generalization about the limits of policy change through science. The main lesson was that time was running out and the federal government could not fail again. Political factors weighed far more heavily in the mind of Congress than scientific ones. Congress did come up with an answer, but the experiences of the 1982 act could have been used far more constructively in reshaping the legislation, especially the potential role that science could play.

Coercive Versus Catalytic Controls

One strategy which legislatures can use in directing bureaucracies is "catalytic control" (Gormley, 1987). This type of action gives direction to a bureaucracy, but, at the same time, allows it considerable flexibility. In contrast, the Yucca Mountain decision is an example of coercive control. The law required DOE to drop its current assessment process and restrict all further analysis to the Nevada site. In doing that, it abandoned the "consultation and cooperation" concept as the basis for resolving differences between the federal government and the states. It substituted political authority for a search for an equitable method of intergovernmental conflict resolution. Could a catalytic orientation to the involvement of the states have been a part of the 1987 amendments? DOE had failed in its implementation of the public involvement provisions of the 1982 act. Nonetheless, the agency's ineffectiveness does not mean the concept is bankrupt. Implemented in a different way, it could contribute to settling the differences between the states and the federal government.

THE NUCLEAR WASTE POLICY ACT AMENDMENTS OF 1987

The search for a politically workable answer is the best way to characterize the 1987 actions taken by Congress to remedy the failures of nuclear waste policy. Congress rarely makes a decision without reference to political feasibility, so the Yucca Mountain decision is not unique. However, the decision is unusual in the extent to which Congress acted without regard to many of the basic concepts which guided its past actions.

The 1987 act was an amendment to the NWPA. The latter legislation offered the potential to resolve what had become an intergovernmental conflict of major proportions (Kearney and Garey, 1982; Downey, 1985). For the first time, the federal government tried to comprehensively address the many pieces of the nuclear waste problem: siting, scheduling, and operation of a repository; the geological properties of a disposal site; economic and legal liability for the wastes; environmental assessment and the role of public involvement (Clary, 1992).

DOE's implementation failures in these areas are well documented (Clary and Kraft, 1989; Jacob, 1990). The effect of the selection process implemented under the NWPA was to undermine the scientific credibility of DOE. The states also became convinced that the agency was not committed to a serious role for them. Within six months, the three states chosen for site characterization studies had filed lawsuits dealing with the conduct of the assessment process and the rights of the states to participate in it. In public hearings held by the agency, virtually all aspects of the methodological process were criticized. Nonetheless, the act signaled a major departure from the past. In the preamble, Congress clearly acknowledged the deficiencies of the federal government's approach to high-level nuclear waste disposal. In terms of Gormley's concept of institutional action as being either remedial or opportunistic, it had elements of the latter.

DOE's implementation of the NWPA fell far short of realizing the opportunistic elements of the legislation. Yet, Yucca Mountain was not the only alternative open to Congress. It could have maintained, and even increased, the role of science and the public in the siting process. The 1982 act was dismissed because of DOE's implementation of it. That does not mean, however, that the concepts and values represented in the NWPA were wrong.

In the 1987 amendments, Congress simply mandated that Yucca Mountain would be the location. Environmental assessment and citizen involvement would still occur, but now only after the fact. Instead of these activities contributing to the choice of the best site among several, they would be used only for the purposes of proving that the Yucca Mountain site was unsuitable. In effect, Congress reversed the process of decisionmaking. The choice shifted from finding the best site to proving one was unacceptable.

The major advocate of the Yucca Mountain approach was Senator Bennett Johnston of Louisiana. His first plan emerged in August 1987. As a longtime supporter of nuclear energy, he wanted to speed up the siting process. The industry was increasingly fearful that if a site was not quickly identified, a repository would not be built in time to solve the crisis of on-site space (at nuclear reactors) for the storage of waste material. Johnston's goal was to remedy their problem, not to solve the underlying scientific and political problems of locating a repository. The one-site strategy avoided the political problem of finding a state willing to accept a repository.

By November 1987, Johnston, chair of the Senate Appropriations Subcommittee on Energy, had successfully attached his bill to the fiscal 1988 energy and water appropriations legislation. Brock Adams of Washington voiced strong opposition, despite the obvious advantages of the Johnston bill to his state (it was no longer under consideration). He characterized the attachment of the bill to an appropriations measure as an "end run" around the committees which should be authorizing such legislation. He further argued that it "destroyed the consensus that we had on nuclear-waste policy beginning in 1982" (Davis, 1987a:2815).

As the vote approached in December, Nevada representatives viewed the Johnston alternative as nothing short of war on the state. One Nevada representative said the bill "will turn our state into a feudal colony." The title of the Johnston bill was the Nuclear Waste Policy Amendments Act of 1987 (in H.R. 3545, Omnibus Budget Reconciliation Act of 1987, Pub. L. 100–203). The bill included provisions dealing with the interim storage of waste (referred to as a monitored retrievable storage), a technical review panel, and compensation to the state of Nevada. None of these sections mitigated the concern of those opposed to the amendments. The critical issue was the designation, by fiat, of Nevada as the final site. Reflecting on the outcome, Ron Wyden, House member from Oregon, said: "This country's in trouble as long as political buy-offs are relied on rather than good science" (Wald, 1987).

AN OPPORTUNISTIC, INFORMAL, AND CATALYTIC NUCLEAR WASTE POLICY

The final 1987 amendments were a classic example of what Gormley calls a "remedial, formal, and coercive" reform of the governmental process. The operative goal was to solve the problem of disposing of nuclear waste in as rapid and politically feasible a manner as possible. The underlying issues, especially the reasons for the intense political conflict between the federal government and the states, were all but ignored.

The legislation was coercive and highly formalistic. It substituted political power for a process of scientific analysis and public involvement as the basis of decisionmaking. Despite the many problems evident in DOE's implementation of the environmental assessment process, cross-site comparison has considerable scientific merit. It allowed for the investigation of different geological media and comparison of sites to each other. By restricting the analysis to Yucca Mountain, determination of the environmental acceptability of a site changed significantly.

When several sites are investigated the question is, which one performs best as measured against a set of evaluatory criteria and against each other? With just one site, the only determination is whether the site minimally meets the criteria. The one-site procedure is methodologically weaker since only one basis of comparison is made: project against criteria instead of project against criteria and other projects.

Comparative evaluation is also important when there is uncertainty about the validity of data. In the Yucca Mountain case, much of the information will be collected through simulation modeling, not empirical investigation of the site. Modeling is often the only possible approach, but that does not remove validity problems. An advantage of investigating alternatives is that site decisions are not dependent upon one source of information. This issue is particularly significant for Yucca Mountain since limited scientific data exist on groundwater movement within the unsaturated zone, the area where the repository will be located. Since the other two sites in the West (prior to the 1987 amendments) were proposed for different geological environments, they did not have this specific data problem. A three-site assessment allows for comparison across locations in terms of the quality of data on geologic, hydrological, and other natural processes. This validity procedure cannot be employed in a one-site approach.

Congress, in abandoning comparative site evaluation, seemed to be only concerned with avoiding, as much as possible, the methodological problems inherent in assessing different sites. These problems are significant, but DOE's implementation of assessment procedures and use of the resulting information were important contributing factors as well. For example, in the first round of siting under the 1982 act, DOE selected Yucca Mountain, Deaf Smith County (Texas), and Hanford (Washington) as the final sites. But in its environmental assessment, they were ranked, respectively, as the first, third, and fifth most preferred sites (U.S. DOE, 1986).

By restricting further investigation to one site, Congress rejected "consultation and cooperation," the basis of public involvement in the siting process in the 1982 act. The concept had shortcomings and its specific meaning had been debated since legislation was first considered in the late 1970s (Varanini, 1982). It was never fully clear what was meant by the term when the NWPA was passed. What would be the specific roles played by the states and tribes at the various stages of the siting process? DOE's actions did very little to clarify this issue; in fact, its handling of public involvement significantly contributed to the eroding public credibility toward the repository program. Nonetheless, the original idea signaled the legislative intent of Congress to try and construct a process of conflict resolution which could mediate the differences between the states and the federal government. In the 1987 amendments, the concept was no longer relevant. The bill forced compliance and Nevada was named as the only site, without negotiation of a mutually acceptable solution to site location.

In an application of game theory to the NIMBY phenomenon, John Gillroy (1990) conceptualizes the conflict in terms of an "assurance game." Within this context, individuals are not necessarily risk adverse, but want their concerns to be treated as legitimate by decisionmakers. Government must empower citizens so they can engage in trusting, cooperative behaviors. The opposite usually occurs so the siting process comes to resemble a "prisoner's dilemma game." The result is that each side pursues its own self-interest to the detriment of achieving an outcome that benefits both parties. Amoral, noncooperative attitudes dominate interaction.

The Yucca Mountain decision shifted public participation from a potential assurance game, as represented by the "consultation and cooperation" concept in the 1982 act, to a prisoner's dilemma. The only possible outcome was the state of Nevada's interests directly pitted against that of the federal government. The decision closed out options which might have shifted the role of citizen involvement to one of cooperation, where mutually acceptable solutions could be sought by citizens and government alike. It narrowed the scope of public involvement since the preliminary site decision had already been made. One of four criteria that Daniel Fiorino (1990) uses to evaluate the effective involvement of citizens in risk decisions is whether a mechanism allows for equality of participation between administrators and the public. The Yucca Mountain decision foreclosed the search for such an alternative. Nevada began the process, so to speak, with two strikes against it.

The legislation could have been written in a very different way. Instead of a remedial approach, Congress could have focused on the opportunities for institutional reform. Emphasis could have been given to flexible approaches that allowed for the development of needed scientific credibility and methods of conflict resolution. What would such an alternative have looked like?

THE UDALL BILL

The major opponent to the one-site approach was Morris Udall, House representative from Arizona. A strong supporter of the 1982 act, he thought it was a fair and permanent solution to the problem of nuclear waste. When the 1987 decision suspended the search for a site in the Midwest and East, Udall lost confidence in the process. He accused the administration of playing politics with the repository program. In his opinion, the White House wanted to protect Republican senators in the upcoming November elections from voter backlash because of the mishandling of the siting program (although many elected Democrats faced the same problem as well).

Udall was the sponsor (along with fifty-five cosponsors) of a bill that would have suspended the 1982 NWPA (H.R. 2967, The Nuclear Waste Policy Amendments of 1987). It stands in marked contrast to the Johnston approach and its reliance upon political power to solve the nuclear waste gridlock. The purpose of the bill was to set up a process through which the failures of the past could be understood and a successful program developed.

The Udall bill established an independent commission to study the sequence of events leading to the obvious failures of the 1982 act. Three members would sit on the commission and have the responsibility of examining new approaches to the waste question. The commission had the power to conduct studies which it felt were necessary. Its mandate included consideration of a second repository, an MRS (monitored retrievable storage) facility, and alternative disposal technologies. The committee was also instructed to address whether DOE should run the program, the order in which the three final sites should be studied, and whether more scientific oversight of the repository program was required. Exploratory drilling at the three final Western sites was prohibited during the six months of the committee's deliberation.

Underlying all the recommendations was a concern with the scientific quality of the research and DOE's credibility as the lead agency. The importance of examining institutional alternatives is critical to resolution of any NIMBY impasse (Rabe, 1991). In a successful siting process in Alberta, Canada, a pivotal factor was the creation of a government corporation to provide direct oversight of facility operation. The establishment of an authority separates it from past governmental actions, which are often failures and the target of public mistrust. For these reasons, an independent high-level radioactive waste authority has long been advocated in the United States (Walker et al., 1983:199–204). The Udall bill, with its opportunistic rather than remedial focus, allowed for the examination of this course of action.

The Udall bill also proposed the creation of a special high-level federal negotiator who had the responsibility of developing an agreement with any state willing to take a repository. This proposal recognized the importance of public acceptance in the successful location of a repository. As described by Joseph Davis (1987c:2478), the basic thinking behind Udall's alternative was "stopping the program, rethinking it and then rebuilding it from the ground up."

An explicit dimension of the Udall bill was the need for reconceptualization of nuclear waste policy in the United States. The past had been plagued with failure. A critical examination of what went wrong must be done. If such an analysis was conducted, what conclusions might have resulted about future directions? A 1990 study by the National Research Council provides some insight into how such a program might be structured. Although it was completed after the Yucca Mountain decision, the conclusions apply equally well to the nuclear waste program before that decision was made.

A MODEL NUCLEAR WASTE PROGRAM

The National Research Council document is entitled "Rethinking High-Level Radioactive Waste Disposal," a clear statement about the direction which future policy development should take. The report criticized DOE for a lack of flexibility, or to use Gormley's concept, the absence of catalytic elements in the management program. DOE, in the council's opinion, is too wedded to a strategy of quantitative, long-range prediction. This strategy has major shortcomings due to a lack of knowledge about crucial dimensions of repository operation and geologic processes. Additionally, the demanding timelines which Congress imposed work against the development of necessary, baseline scientific information.

A preferred approach would be recognition of the inherent uncertainty in developing a repository. An exploratory research program would be designed. Its main goal would be to increase understanding of the many questions related to technological, environmental, and health risks. No single data source would suffice. Confidence would be increased through the application of a variety of techniques including engineering design experiments, mathematical modeling, performance assessment, and experience with similar natural environments where radioactive materials are present. Bringing these different sources of knowledge together could have a catalytic effect, allowing for a synthesis of data on a broad range of issues related to the operation of a repository and its impact on the environment. DOE's present emphasis on quantitative modeling is much narrower, leaving little room to learn from experience.

Brian Cook and his colleagues (1990) argue that a new scientific approach also requires a change in organizational design or, in Gormley's terms, that institutional opportunities must be explored. An adaptive strategy of repository location and management is needed. An organizational culture of learning must be adopted. DOE has to examine its emphasis on centralized bureaucratic control. Flexibility has to be given to line personnel to allow them to respond to uncertain situations, which will inevitably arise in the siting and operation of a repository. The agency has to broaden its definition of what constitutes the problem of radioactive waste management. A strongly technocratic orientation must be replaced by one that gives greater weight to factors of a socioeconomic nature. It will not suffice for the agency to pursue a solely technical agenda when radioactive waste has high political and social salience to the general public.

Unlike the Yucca Mountain decision, the Udall bill and other alternatives make no presuppositions about how to proceed. Instead of a remedial, formal, and coercive approach that specifies the final site, the emphasis is on building an exploratory and flexible process that can meet scientific and public scrutiny. In doing that, these strategies have far more promise to resolve the issues underlying the NIMBY dimensions of this siting conflict.

YUCCA MOUNTAIN: A PRESCRIPTION FOR CONTINUED GRIDLOCK ?

The Yucca Mountain decision has significance beyond the disposal of high-level nuclear waste. Is it a model that may be used by states as they seek to resolve the gridlocks they face in locating hazardous, toxic, and low-level radioactive waste facilities? (Hadden et al., 1983; Bord, 1985; Heiman, 1990). Will the federal government again resort to political criteria, if and when another nuclear waste repository has to be sited? The Nevada decision has precedents at the state level. By 1987, thirty-six states

had enacted siting laws which shifted final authority from local governments to the state (Mazmanian and Morell, 1988).

Yucca Mountain and related state-level initiatives raise important questions about democratic decisionmaking and environmental politics. What
is the legitimate exercise of political authority to resolve siting controversies? For high-level nuclear waste, Congress chose to abandon a process
of political participation and science in searching for a final site. Instead,
it simply mandated the location. In doing so, it made authority the basis
of decisionmaking. It was certainly a legal action for Congress to take, but
was it a wise one? By constructing a siting process with only one candidate,
it could circumvent the NIMBY reaction so prominent in the states.
However, the costs may be an increase in environmental risks and erosion
of the already low public credibility toward the program.

If this decision serves as a model for other federal decisions or state
governments facing similar choices, it is a questionable precedent. An
authoritative decision does not address the underlying concerns which
citizens have about a site "in their backyard." Behind this kind of policy
choice is a negative view of the public and its role in the assessment of
technological and environmental risks. This attitude stands in marked
contrast to the National Environmental Policy Act of 1969, where public
involvement was seen as critical to the maintenance of environmental
values (Caldwell, 1982).

In supporting Johnston's alternative, Congress apparently accepted the
conventional portrayal of the NIMBY syndrome: citizens are uninformed,
emotional, and unwilling to listen to any other position than their own
(Glaberson, 1988). However, not all contemporary observers of NIMBY
agree. Instead, they argue that citizen fears are often well founded (Morell
and Magorian, 1982; Elliott, 1984; Freudenburg, 1987; Kraft and Clary,
1991).

They cite a variety of evidence for their position. Many hazardous waste
facilities have failed to contain toxic materials and leaked them to the
environment. The risks of living nearby are frequently unclear. Adjacent
residents have developed health problems at rates substantially higher than
the general population. Experts repeatedly disagree or present evidence
that is ambiguous or even contradictory. Under these circumstances, they
claim, public opposition is hardly irrational.

A "Yucca Mountain" type decision solves the problem of where to locate
a facility. It does not establish a process whereby such a decision, in the
future, is made in a democratic and equitable manner and reflects sound
scientific judgment. The same underlying issues may re-emerge when
government makes another siting decision.

CONCLUSION : A DEMOCRATIC ALTERNATIVE TO YUCCA MOUNTAIN

The siting of risky facilities is a case study in how to balance the conflicting demands of technology, citizen participation, and political authority. Political philosophers have addressed this broader question and their conclusions have significant implications for the resolution of siting controversies. A noted critical theorist, Jurgen Habermas (1970), argues that technology rests on a concept of action for a purpose. As such, it exists to solve problems, a means to an end. In this context, technology does not pose a threat to society. The dilemma is the extent to which the technological perspective comes to dominate societal approaches to problems. Often, a "technical fix" is pervasive, the attitude that all problems are simply a matter of finding the correct technological answer.

The political consequences of the instrumental view of problem solving are significant. It results in the dominance of the expert in decisionmaking. Values that do not easily fit into the technological paradigm are de-emphasized or ignored altogether. Habermas is particularly concerned about the role of citizens in this decisionmaking context. Their perceptions, attitudes, and opinions are grounded on a very different system of knowledge than the technical system of the engineer and other practitioners of modern technology. The public policy challenge is the reconciliation of the disparate values embodied in these alternative views of the world.

Habermas's solution is an interactional concept of social action. A decision should result from all the parties to an issue reaching a consensus, not simply the outcome of the techniques used in analyzing a problem. In contrast, the Yucca Mountain decision reflects the instrumental dimension. Research will be done in the form of environmental assessments, but simply to achieve a particular end, the location of a repository. The broader concept of using science to assess alternative sites in the context of a process of "consultation and cooperation," as the 1982 act set out, is abandoned.

The proposed alternatives to the Yucca Mountain decision are quite different. They are not based on the premise of the separation of instrumental and interactional approaches, but instead fundamentally link them. Citizen participation in siting decisions is crucial, so broader, social values become part of decisionmaking. Equally important is a credible base of information on which to base choices. Regardless of the form of participation, sound data must exist. Without it, NIMBY behaviors are inevitable. Meaningful participation ultimately depends upon the trust that citizens have of project data presented to them (Bella et al., 1988; Elliott, 1984).

Proponents of risky facilities must understand the central role that knowledge plays in the siting process. It not only serves the instrumental purpose of assessing environmental and health risk, but also is the basis of interaction between government and citizen. Too often, agencies use assessment for only instrumental purposes (Taylor, 1984). They ignore the role assessment can play in facilitating positive citizen involvement. Assessment established the framework of trust necessary for a constructive dialogue among parties to the issue. The artificial separation of science from the political process serves to undermine the legitimacy of decision-making. Thus, Senator Johnston's closing summary of the Yucca Mountain decision may be far off the mark: "I think it's fair to say we've solved the nuclear waste problem with this legislation. The problem with nuclear waste has never been scientific, it's always been emotional and political" (Rasky, 1987).

Johnston won the battle; the Yucca Mountain alternative passed Congress. He may win the war: a high-level nuclear waste facility may be located there. However, the fundamental scientific and democratic issues of siting remain unresolved. Until a bridging of science and politics occurs, an equitable means of making this decision will continue to elude the U.S. political system.

REFERENCES

Andrews, Richard L. and Terrence K. Pierson. 1985. Local Control or State Override: Experiences and Lessons to Date. *Policy Studies Journal*, 14:90–99.

Barke, Richard. 1985. Policy Learning and the Evolution of Federal Hazardous Waste Policy. *Policy Studies Journal*, 14:123–131.

Bella, David A., Charles D. Mosher, and Stephen N. Calvo. 1988. Establishing Trust: Nuclear Waste Disposal. *Journal of Professional Issues in Engineering*, 114 (January):40–50.

Bord, Richard. 1985. Problems in Siting Low Level Radioactive Wastes: A Focus on Public Participation. In S. K. Majumdar and E. Willard Miller, eds. *Management of Radioactive Materials and Wastes: Issues and Progress*. Philadelphia: Pennsylvania Academy of Science, 189–215.

Caldwell, Lynton K. 1982. *Science and the National Environmental Policy Act*. University, AL: University of Alabama Press.

Carter, Luther J. 1987. *Nuclear Imperatives and Public Trust: Dealing with Radioactive Waste*. Washington, DC: Resources for the Future.

Clary, Bruce B. 1992. The Passage of the Nuclear Waste Policy Act of 1982: A Multiple Perspectives Explanation. *Policy Studies Review*, 10, 4:90–102.

Clary, Bruce B. and Michael E. Kraft. 1989. Environmental Assessment, Science, and Policy Failure: The Politics of Nuclear Waste Disposal. In Robert Barlett, ed. *Policy Through Impact Assessment*. Westport, CT: Greenwood.

Cook, Brian, Jacque L. Emel, and Roger E. Kasperson. 1990. Organizing and Managing Radioactive Waste Disposal As an Experiment. *Journal of Policy Analysis and Management*, 8, 3:339–366.

Davis, Joseph A. 1987a. Nevada Struggling to Fend Off Nuclear Dump. *Congressional Quarterly*, November 14:2815.

——. 1987b. Nevada To Get Nuclear Waste: Everyone Else "Off the Hook." *Congressional Quarterly*, December 19:3136–3137.

——. 1987c. Udall Urges New Study of Nuclear-Waste Issue. *Congressional Quarterly*, October 10:2478–2479.

Delogu, Orlando E. 1990. "NIMBY" Is a National Environmental Problem. *South Dakota Law Review*, 35:198–219.

Downey, Gary L. 1985. Federalism and Nuclear Waste Disposal: The Struggle over Shared Decision Making. *Journal of Policy Analysis and Management*, 5:73–99.

Elliott, Michael L. Poirier. 1984. Improving Community Acceptance of Hazardous Waste Facilities Through Alternative Systems for Mitigating and Managing Risk. *Hazardous Waste*, 1:397–410.

Fiorino, Daniel J. 1990. Citizen Participation and Environmental Risk: A Survey of Institutional Mechanisms. *Science, Technology and Human Values*, 15:226–243.

Freudenburg, William R. 1987. Rationality and Irrationality in Estimating the Risks of Nuclear Waste Disposal. Paper presented at Waste Management '87, Tucson, AZ.

Gillroy, John Martin. 1990. Moral Considerations and Public Policy Choice: Individual Autonomy and the NIMBY Problem. Paper presented at the Annual Meeting of the Midwest Political Science Association, Chicago, April.

Glaberson, William. 1988. Coping in the Age of "Nimby." *New York Times*, June 19, sec. 3, p. 1.

Gormley, William T. 1987. Institutional Policy Analysis: A Critical Review. *Journal of Policy Analysis and Management*, 6:153–169.

Habermas, Jurgen. 1970. *Toward a Rational Society*. Boston: Beacon Press.

Hadden, Susan G., Joan Veillette, and Thomas Brandt. 1983. State Roles in Siting Hazardous Waste Disposal Facilities: From State Preemption to Local Veto. In James P. Lester and Ann O'M. Bowman, eds. *The Politics of Hazardous Waste Management*. Durham, NC: Duke University Press.

Heiman, Michael. 1990. Using Public Authorities to Site Hazardous Waste Management Facilities: Problems and Prospects. *Policy Studies Journal*, 18:974–985.

Jacob, Gerald. 1990. *Site Unseen: The Politics of Siting a Nuclear Waste Repository*. Pittsburgh: University of Pittsburgh Press.

Kearney, Richard C. and Robert B. Garey. 1982. American Federalism and the Management of Radioactive Wastes. *Public Administration Review*, 42:14–24.

Kraft, Michael E. 1990. Environmental Gridlock: Searching for Consensus in Congress. In Norman J. Vig and Michael E. Kraft, eds. *Environmental Policy in the 1990's*. Washington, DC: Congressional Quarterly, 103–124.

Kraft, Michael E. and Bruce B. Clary. 1991. Citizen Response and the NIMBY Syndrome: Public Response to Radioactive Waste Disposal. *Western Political Quarterly*, 44 (June):299–328.

Malone, Charles R. 1991. High-Level Nuclear Waste Disposal: A Perspective on Technocracy and Democracy. *Growth and Change*, 22:69–74.

Matheny, Albert R. and Bruce A. Williams. 1985. Knowledge vs. NIMBY: Assessing
    Florida's Strategy for Siting Hazardous Waste Disposal Facilities. *Policy Studies
    Journal*, 14:70–80.
Mazmanian, Daniel and David Morell. 1988. The Elusive Pursuit of Toxics Management.
    The Public Interest, 90:81–98.
Morell, David and Christopher Magorian. 1982. *Siting Hazardous Waste Facilities: Local
    Opposition and the Myth of Preemption*. Cambridge, MA: Ballinger.
National Research Council, Commission on Geosciences, Environment, and Resources.
    1990. *Rethinking High-Level Radioactive Waste Disposal: A Position Statement
    of the Board on Radioactive Waste Management*. Washington, DC: National
    Academy Press.
O'Hare, Michael, Lawrence Bacow, and Debra Sanderson. 1983. *Facility Siting and
    Public Opposition*. New York: Van Nostrand Reinhold.
Rabe, Barry G. 1991. Beyond the NIMBY Syndrome in Hazardous Waste Facility Siting:
    The Albertan Breakthrough and the Prospects for Cooperation in Canada and the
    United States. Governance, 4:184–206.
Rasky, Susan. 1987. Nevada May End Up Holding the Nuclear Bag. *New York Times*,
    December 20, sec. 4, p. 4.
Taylor, Serge. 1984. *Making Bureaucracies Think: The Environmental Impact Statement
    Strategy of Administrative Reform*. Stanford, CA.: Stanford University Press.
U.S. Department of Energy, Office of Civilian Radioactive Waste Management. 1986.
    *Multiattribute Utility Analysis of Sites Nominated for Characterization for the
    First Radioactive-Waste Repository—A Decision-Aiding Methodology*.
    DOE/RW–0074. Washington, DC: Department of Energy, May.
Varanini, E. E., III. 1982. Consultation and Concurrence: Process or Substance. In
    William E. Colglazier, ed. *The Politics of Nuclear Waste*. New York: Pergamon,
    138–159.
Wald, Matthew. 1987. Nevada Is Expected As Congress Choice For Atom Waste Site.
    New York Times, December 15, sec. 1, p. 1.
Walker, Charles A., Leroy C. Gould, and Edward J. Woodhouse. 1983. Value Issues in
    Radioactive Waste Management. In Charles A. Walker, Leroy C. Gould, and
    Edward J. Woodhouse, eds. *Too Hot To Handle? Social and Policy Issues in the
    Management of Radioactive Wastes*. New Haven, CT: Yale University Press,
    184–206.

3

Low-Level Radioactive Waste Compacts: Cases in the Illogic of Collective Action?

MICHAEL V. MCGINNIS

"The waste grows: woe to him who harbors waste."
—F. Nietzsche, *Among Daughters of the Wasteland*

After over forty years of policy stalemate, Congress called on the states to initiate and form interstate compacts to deal with the complex, intractable problem of finding and developing alternative repository sites for low-level radioactive waste (LLRW).[1] Each year approximately 2.7 million cubic feet of LLRW is produced (CSA, 1989:669). The majority of LLRW comes from the nation's 112 commercial nuclear power plants. New York, Pennsylvania, Tennessee, North Carolina, South Carolina, Illinois, Oregon, California, Virginia, and Alabama account for about two-thirds of all the waste produced. Other states such as North Dakota and South Dakota produce less than 5 cubic feet of LLRW per year. The waste may be in solid, liquid, or gaseous form. No technology is proven to secure, isolate, protect, neutralize, and control hazardous LLRW waste.

Three existing federal sites for storing LLRW in Hanford, Washington; Beatty, Nevada; and Barnwell, South Carolina, will close in 1993. With this in mind, Congress passed the Low-Level Radioactive Waste Policy Act of 1980 (LLWPA) and delegated to the states the responsibility of developing alternative waste repositories. Pursuant to the LLWPA, states had the option of either joining an interstate compact or developing their own repository by January 1993. The LLWPA stipulates that compacts develop procedures to safely treat, package, ship, and dispose of the wastes. In 1985, Congress amended the LLWPA to add further incentives for states to find and develop alternative LLRW facilities. The 1985 amendment outlined financial penalties if states failed to develop sites. Also, the amendment incorporated a "take title clause" whereby states would assume legal liability for their own wastes.[2] As of June 1993, most of the proposed state compacts had been legally agreed upon and tentative host-site states designated. However, despite the LLWPA as amended, no LLRW compact has yet to agree on where specifically to dispose of their wastes, and a majority of commercial waste remains at reactor sites.

Several scholars and waste management professionals maintain that LLRW compacts represent a promising solution to a serious national problem (Smiley, 1984; Kearney, 1988; Kearney and Stucker, 1985; Jordan et al., 1984; Riggs, 1990). However, the use of the LLRW compact to deal with hazardous wastes is unique and extraordinary. The LLRW compact process represents the first time the states have attempted to use the compact as a vehicle to govern a commodity that has been a part of national interstate commerce (Kearney and Stucker, 1985). Also, most compacts in the past have been information clearinghouses with little or no authority. The efficacy of the LLRW compact to deal with waste-related problems in a collective fashion remains uncertain and requires further analysis.

In this chapter, I review the LLRW compacts as conduits of collective action. I suggest that cooperative behavior among LLRW compact members is a function of the following key factors: a high level of regional authority, a high level of regional interdependence, a diffusion of costs and benefits, and a movement away from a technocratic approach in decision-making. If LLRW compacts are to encompass the diverse and often conflicting interests which exist in the policymaking process, an open approach to administration is necessary.

INTERSTATE RELATIONSHIPS

In the United States, there are two different types of interstate relationships, *vertical* and *horizontal*. Vertical relationships typically involve an active federal government participant—indeed, the federal government may well have organized the regional commission. For example, a federal-state compact is a hierarchical administrative mechanism insofar as states are *subordinate* to the federal government (Grad, 1963). In such a relationship, there is the possibility of parties appealing decisions made in the framework of the commission to the relevant federal agency. Such an appeal may act as a barrier to consensus building.

Horizontal regionalism is essentially a lateral, nonhierarchical, relatively autonomous voluntary relationship between states. There is no formal representation of the federal government's interest in this relationship. However, the federal government is often an influential participant. LLRW compacts are an example of nonhierarchical suppliers of public goods. Despite the fact that the federal government is not a formal member of LLRW compacts, the Department of Energy's (DOE) Low-Level Waste Management Program has helped catalyze state and regional programs by: lending staff to several states for policy and technical planning; supporting regional compact negotiations with grants and staff support; participation in state-sponsored public information forums; collecting data on waste generation and management for use by states; and participating in and contributing to other state efforts such as hearings, development of state plans, and the like.

The use of either the vertical or horizontal compact appears to correspond with the shifts in the role of the states in policymaking. Between 1950 and 1970 the rate of compact adoption accelerated to more than four a year (Nice, 1987:70). During this period, the rise in the use of the interstate compact may be a result of the new dimension of state power in intergovernmental relations. After 1970, the rate of growth fell dramatically (CSG, 1977). This decline can be understood partly as a response to the centralization of policymaking at the federal level (Beer, 1973). In the 1980s, the Reagan administration began to look increasingly to the states as policy innovators. It cut grants-in-aid for environmental projects (Davies, 1984; Lester, 1986) and delegated responsibility for developing environmental policy to the states (Davis and Lester, 1987; Fitzgerald et al., 1988). Perhaps Reagan's New Federalism may lead to a revival in the use of the interstate compact (Chi, 1990).

LLRW compacts represent a departure from the traditional use of the administrative device and have been delegated a significant level of authority by the federal government. In addition, LLRW compacts contend with similar problems facing the Energy Research and Development Administration and the DOE and their attempt to build and open the Waste Isolation Pilot Plant (WIPP) in southeastern New Mexico.[3] In general, LLRW compacts represent a test of the vitality of the states and their ability to develop important environmental policy.

LLRW COMPACTS: DEALING WITH COLLECTIVE BADS

There has been little if any contemporary analysis of the interstate compact as an administrative conduit of collective action. In her comprehensive evaluation of interstate arrangements, Martha Derthick (1974:13) shows that, for the most part, compacts need authority and to encompass "externalities" (avoid spillover and internalize diverse interests) to be effective. Overall, she maintains that the odds are against regional agencies flourishing. In addition, Ann Bowman (1985:139–140) suggests that "regionalism seems to flourish when the stakes are low and when there is no perception of winners and losers." In LLRW compact administration there are potential winners and losers. Consequently, one might expect that LLRW compacts will find cooperation problematic.

In *The Logic of Collective Action*, Mancur Olson (1965) suggests that through cooperation small groups are more able to resolve their collective action problems. Self-interested individuals will not join large organizations unless they are coerced to participate or offered "selective" incentives (tangible in nature). Because of the number of potential benefactors and the nature of the collective bad (the counterpart to collective goods), LLRW compacts face barriers to cooperation often found in large groups, for example, free riders and the need to offer selective incentives and encompass various externalities.

There remains some disagreement over what factors are required to remedy the shortcomings of decentralized choice. Scholars have emphasized the need for coercion. For example, Garrett Hardin (1968) envisions a "tragedy of the commons" whereby a system without centralized authority or what he calls "mutual coercion" would end in disaster because individuals would seek to maximize their marginal utility of a shared resource. Other scholars question the role of coercion in sustaining cooperation (Axelrod, 1986). In an analysis of collective bads, Matthew Crenson (1987:269) argues that coercion may not be a fundamental function of cooperative behavior, and maintains that coercion "is a notoriously ineffective means of achieving compliance."

In the case of LLRW compacts, governmental "coercion" (in the guise of the congressional mandates and incentives found in the LLWPA) has not sustained cooperation between key participants (Condon, 1990). Perhaps one reason federal incentives have not sustained cooperation rests in the severe nature of the collective bad, LLRW. The LLRW produced by nuclear fission is the dirtiest form of waste we have ever had to deal with for it remains "dangerous" for hundreds of years. LLRW will remain a collective bad for generations to come, and is, in essence, intergenerational. One of the fundamental ethical dilemmas associated with LLRW is exporting the risks to future generations.[4] Imposing the financial and medical-related debts and possible irreversible environmental damage which might be caused by the waste on future generations is ethically suspect (Kasperson, 1983).[5] To deal with the problem *today*, administrators face the by-products of the collective bad and must contend with various economic constraints and political barriers.

There are important economic concerns. There is some doubt whether multiple small compacts can be economically viable as waste volumes diminish or stabilize. Existing LLRW facilities can dispose of wastes at an average cost of $33 per cubic foot. To pay for the disposal of LLRW at a new site, costs per cubic foot have been estimated as high as $500 (Kearney, 1989:234). Moreover, it may cost up to $40 million to develop a new site (ibid.). Although a majority of the costs of developing and operating a new facility will come from waste producers, some environmental groups and state representatives are worried that the costs related to cleaning up "leaks" would come from taxpayers. This has prevented the development of several proposed facilities. From a fiscal point of view, states may find it difficult to develop their repositories.

In addition to ethical and economic concerns, LLRW compacts must deal with the fears of the public. Guided by the not-in-my-backyard (NIMBY) syndrome, many LLRW compacts are composed of representatives who are attempting to keep the wastes outside of their political jurisdictions. Conflict between various member states is the norm, and the negotiation process is continually being interrupted. In addition to the NIMBY syndrome, LLRW compacts face other barriers to collective action. This chapter will focus on some of the administrative characteristics necessary for participants in LLRW compact policymaking to cooperate.

FUNCTIONS OF COOPERATION IN LLRW COMPACTS

Since 1980, several states have entered into interstate compacts for the disposal of LLRW (see Table 3.1). After reviewing several cases of LLRW compacts, four key functions of cooperative behavior have been identified.

The Allocation of Costs and Benefits

Different patterns of costs and benefits influence the decisionmaking situation because decisions often require consent or concurrence on the part of those interests who bear the crux of the costs. (This is consistent with a wide range of work on bureaucracy, e.g., Wilson, 1974.) Different patterns of costs and benefits arising from the problem of where to dispose of LLRW will affect how the compact agencies work. Each state participating in a compact has to balance the interests of the local population bearing the costs against the interest of the region which receives the

Table 3.1
LLW Compact Groupings

Compact	Members
Central States	Arkansas, Oklahoma, Nebraska, Louisiana, Kansas
Central Midwest	Illinois, Kentucky
Southwest	California, Arizona, North Dakota, South Dakota
Midwest	Wisconsin, Indiana, Iowa, Ohio, Minnesota, Missouri
Southeast	Georgia, Florida, Alabama, Tennessee, North Carolina, South Carolina, Mississippi, Virginia
Northwest	Idaho, Washington, Montana, Hawaii, Oregon, Alaska, Utah
Rocky Mountain	Colorado, Nevada, New Mexico, Wyoming
Appalachian	Pennsylvania, Delaware, Maryland, West Virginia
Northeast	Connecticut, New Jersey
Independent	Texas, New York, Massachusetts
Unaligned	Rhode Island, Vermont, New Hampshire, Maine, Michigan

benefits. The distribution of "public goods" to the region and the concentration of "collective bads" in the local area is unique to LLRW compacts (Kearney and Stucker, 1985). As Paul Furiga (1989:50) writes, "[Compacts] face the necessity of healing regional differences, coming up with millions of dollars for the dumps and at the same time allaying the fears of citizens." In general, deciding where LLRW should be disposed of is as much a political problem as a technological one (Kasperson, 1991).

Public fears pertaining to radioactive waste are well documented (Carter, 1987; Weart, 1988; Pijawka and Mushkatel, 1992) and need to be accounted for in decisionmaking. Reconciling the demands of waste disposal with their environmental risks and the NIMBY syndrome is one particular obstacle facing LLRW compacts (Kraft and Clary, 1991; Erikson, 1990). Public fear leads to distrust of public officials, and has incited an uncompromising opposition by citizens to agency decisions (Bella et al., 1988). How the compact allocates the costs and benefits and encompasses the local interests is one function of cooperative behavior.

The political controversies in the southeast and midwest compacts are examples of what the other compacts will face. Since it had been designated to receive waste from other states, citizen and legislative support was building for North Carolina to withdraw from the southeast compact (Kearney, 1989). Critics claimed that the designation process was biased against North Carolina. The midwest compact faced a similar NIMBY-related problem. Michigan, the designated host state, did not consent to accepting other states' waste, and for myriad reasons eventually withdrew from the compact. Ohio has stepped in as the host state. Indeed, concentrating the collective bads has led to conflict between the designated state and the other compact members.

States who do withdraw from a compact and decide to go it alone face several serious problems (other than those that interstate compacts face). First, since a single state does not constitute a compact, the state might be required by Congress to accept out-of-state wastes. Second, it takes four to five years to identify, construct, and license a facility to dispose of LLRW, and the particular state will incur the costs of such a process. For instance, New York does not expect to have an LLRW facility until at least 1998. In addition, states who are not members of a compact have the same administrative, operational, and political needs of interstate compacts. For example, Texas, an independent state, has found it difficult to find an acceptable repository site. Texas wanted its LLRW to be disposed of in the Chihuahua Desert, but a judge decided that the proposed site was too close to the Rio Grande, El Paso, underground aquifers, and historic Indian petroglyphs. States which are not members of a compact do not escape requirements for issue resolution even in embarking on an independent nuclear waste disposal program.

Overall, both LLRW compacts and noncompact states have found it difficult to make compensation payments to the local citizenry and compel agreement. In an attempt to reconcile NIMBY-related concerns, the northeast compact (made up of Connecticut and New Jersey) developed a comprehensive compensation and incentive package for the local citizenry (Riggs, 1990:82). The compensation package includes some of the following: a percentage of the facility's gross receipts, a mitigation agreement not to exceed $150,000, a payment in lieu of taxes provision, and a property value guarantee program. Also, the Connecticut Hazardous Waste Management Service developed a citizen board to deal with citizen concerns in the siting process, and held a series of public education meetings to present information on the risks related to the development of a new facility. Despite such efforts, Connecticut and the northeast compact have not been able to successfully overcome problems related to NIMBY and have had to settle on a repository site at the Millstone Nuclear Power Complex.[6]

Compact Authority

Compact authority as granted by the federal government matters more in situations with difficult cost/benefit trade-offs such as those found in LLRW compact administration. Compact authority involves two potentially separable issues. First, authority is greater if the participants in the compact agency make a final decision that cannot be appealed to another governmental level (e.g., the federal government or state legislature). If there are veto points in the process, compact authority is threatened. Second, authority increases if the compact has the power to enforce its decisions. Compacts need "implementation teeth" to enforce decisions made. Authority increases if other actors are required by law to acknowledge the decisions reached in the agency and regard them as binding.

In an insightful analysis on the constitutional problems facing noncompact states who decide to dispose of wastes on their own, David Condon (1990:71) suggests that Congress "created strong incentives for those regional compacts and states without disposal sites to locate, license, and construct disposal facilities." The LLWPA stipulates that states can either join a compact or may have to receive wastes *from other states*. Compact membership is a way of avoiding federal pre-emption in deciding where wastes should be disposed of. If states do not join compacts and decide to go it alone, the noncompact state, according to Condon (1990:85) "is not likely to be able to [legally] prohibit the importation of out-of-state low-level waste." By delegating authority to compact states, Congress hopes to spawn compact formation.

Cooperation among LLRW compact participants remains elusive. Perhaps one reason is the ambiguity of compact authority. Condon (1990) suggests that if Congress grants exclusionary authority to noncompact states such as New York and Texas, the authority of compact states would be undermined. Also, compact states need the authority to keep noncompact waste outside of their chosen repository, and thereby avoid free riders and spillover.

A case in point is the southwest compact (made up of California, Arizona, North Dakota, and South Dakota). The southwest compact may be the *first* compact to develop and operate a waste facility (*Nuclear News*, 1988). An initial repository site near Ward Valley, California, was agreed on by compact members. The terms of the compact call for the other significant LLRW generator, Arizona, to develop a site that would succeed the Ward Valley site. California, the dominant member of the compact, has a stake in developing a repository, for the amount of the LLRW produced by nuclear power plants is significant and they have no repository.

Environmentalists, organized into a coalition called "Don't Waste California," are concerned that the proposed California site would become the next national repository, and that noncompact states could begin to use the repository. Fifteen noncompact states expressed interest in using the repository. As a result, the southwest compact formally denied access by noncompact member states to the Ward Valley site, and sent letters to all nonmember states stipulating that the site is to be used only by the compact members. The authority of a compact to deny access remains ambiguous, and will, no doubt, be resolved in the courts (Condon, 1990).[7]

A Sense of Interdependency

If one considers the complex nature of transporting hazardous wastes across state boundaries, a sense of regional efficacy becomes crucial. David Nice (1987:77) defines interdependence as a function of geographic proximity. Interstate compact cooperation increases as the sense of interdependence increases (ibid.). In terms of geographical proximity, some LLRW compacts are not "regional" but separated by one or more states and are "umbrella" organizations (Condon, 1990:70). As compacts evolve and attempt to dispose of their wastes, transporting hazardous materials across noncompact state boundaries to a designated repository site will cause problems. Many states have laws forbidding the transportation of hazardous materials across state lines. LLRW compacts which are "regional" and interdependent will likely be more successful in implementing decisions.

Moving Beyond Technocentrism

In LLRW compacts, allegiance to a technocentric administrative approach will not foster cooperation among contending preferences (McGinnis, 1992). The technocentric ideal, as defined by Tim O'Riordan (1977:4), is an administrative approach which is "suspicious of attempts to widen the basis for participation and lengthy discussion in project appraisal and policy review." The technocratic approach emphasizes a closed decisionmaking process, and is grounded in a faith in bureaucratic expertise, professionalism, and technology to resolve difficult problems.

LLRW compacts which rely on a closed administrative approach have found it difficult to encompass public fears (crystallized in NIMBY) and other environmental interests. For example, environmentalists charge that the southwest compact made the decision to develop the repository in Ward

Valley without public input or debate. They maintain that the decision to develop a California repository was made by only the League of Women Voters, the CalRad Forum (made up of commercial nuclear waste producers), and California's Department of Health. Critics of the Ward Valley site believe that the operational costs of the new site are too great and have been underestimated by the compact. U.S. Ecology (USE), the company the compact has chosen to construct and operate the repository, has had problems in managing past disposal sites (one of USE's federal dumps is now a Superfund site). "Don't Waste California" fears that Californians may be held accountable for potential contamination costs from accidents, and are worried about the potential environmental consequences of the proposed site. They believe that wildlife (including the endangered desert tortoise), the Mojave wilderness area, the Colorado River, and underground aquifers are at risk.

As a result of the potential environmental and cost-related impacts, the California State Lands Commission delayed development of the proposed repository pending further research into potential problems related to the site. The California State Lands Commission must first approve the transfer of federal land to the state before the Ward Valley site is developed. The commission's refusal to approve the transfer represents a potential veto of the compact's decision.[8] Other compacts have faced similar problems in the process of deciding where to dispose of their LLRW.

In the development of LLRW disposal policy, an open administrative approach is necessary. This is consistent with the work of John Dryzek (1987), and Robert Paehlke and Douglas Torgerson (1990). In *Rational Ecology*, Dryzek argues that administered "hierarchies" with rigid command control and centralization are problematic. He (1987:108) maintains that hierarchical administrative types are able to deal with only two kinds of problems: those which are familiar and routine, and those which are unambiguous and tangible. LLRW disposal problems are neither routine or unambiguous. Paehlke and Torgerson (1990:1–13) believe that an environmental administrative process grounded in control and domination is irresponsible and ineffective. They suggest that opening administrative decisionmaking to the public and promoting majoritarian democratic opportunities is key to effective environmental decisionmaking.

There are ways in which the LLRW compact process could be opened. Local interests could be encompassed within decisions by giving them the authority of "consultation and concurrence"—or the authority to veto a compact's plan to develop a waste repository in their local area. Second, a local government representative could be placed on the compact. In the southwest compact, for example, a local representative is a formal voting member. Overall, an open administrative approach will prove more successful in reconciling NIMBY-related concerns and encompassing diverse and often conflicting interests in LLRW policy development.[9]

CONCLUSION

There remain significant problems which need to be reconciled if LLRW compacts are to succeed in developing policy. Dealing with the political "hot" potato of radwaste is predicated on several functions of interstate cooperation. This chapter has focused on four administrative characteristics which will increase the chances for successful siting and operation of LLRW facilities. Further research is warranted in this area for LLRW compacts represent interesting cases in the logic of collective action.

Whether or not LLRW compacts can act as conduits of collective action and actually site repositories remains to be discovered. LLRW represents an innovative attempt to deal with problems associated with the intractable problem. Key participants in LLRW compact policymaking have only just begun to agree on where to dispose of wastes. Federal incentives have not sustained cooperation between key participants. Serious economic, ethical, and political dilemmas remain unaddressed. As compacts evolve and attempt to find and operate disposal facilities, transporting materials across noncompact state boundaries may prove to be another barrier. The ultimate success of the LLRW compacts rests on developing the political, social, and institutional characteristics necessary to deal with myriad concerns.

NOTES

This material is based upon work supported by the National Science Foundation under Award SES–9122122, and the University of California. Any opinions, findings, and conclusions or recommendations expressed in this publication are those of the author and do not necessarily reflect the views of the National Science Foundation or the University of California. I would like to thank Dean Mann, John Woolley, Peter Digeser, James Lima, and Eric Herzik for their useful comments on earlier drafts.

1. Low-level radioactive waste can be defined as all radioactive wastes not classified as high-level, transuranic waste, mill tailings, or by-product materials which incorporate tools for waste treatment materials, filters, sludges, ion exchange resins, and evaporated bottoms from reactor plant systems. There is some debate over how lethal "low-level" waste is, for it is a catch-all category which may include everything except high-level wastes. The half life (or the time it takes for half the atoms of a radioactive element to decay) of the various contents of LLRW may vary from 100 years to over 500 years.

2. The independent state of New York and seventeen other states challenged the LLWPA as an intrusion on state "sovereignty." In *New York v. United States*, No. 91–543, the Supreme Court upheld portions of the LLWPA that provide financial incentives to states to find repository sites for LLRW. However, in a six to three decision, the Court declared unconstitutional the LLWPA's provision that a state was the legal owner of all LLRW within its borders if it was not able to meet its disposal needs by January 1, 1996. Under this "take title" provision, Justice Sandra Day O'Connor (writing for the Court) maintained that "Congress has crossed the line distinguishing encouragement from coercion." O'Connor based her decision on the Tenth Amendment. In general, the Court's decision may force nuclear utilities to expand on existing storage facilities at the reactor sites. In addition, the Court decision maintains state responsibility to provide new LLRW facilities.

3. For a review of problems related to WIPP, see Gary L. Downey, "Federalism and Nuclear Waste Disposal: The Struggle over Shared Decision Making," *Journal of Policy Analysis and Management*, 5, 1 (1985):73–99; and Hank C. Jenkins-Smith, "Alternative Theories of the Policy Process: Reflections on Research for the Study of Nuclear Waste Policy," *Political Science and Politics*, 24, 2 (June 1991):157–166.

4. In light of the intergenerational nature of LLRW, Alvin Weinberg suggests that a "priesthood" or a "permanent cadre of experts" is required to guard the reactors and the waste to assure their safety over time (see Weinberg, "Technology and Ecology—Is There a Need for Confrontation," *Bioscience*, 23 (1973):41–46). The DOE is considering such a technological priesthood to deal with high-level radioactive wastes.

5. In addition to the intergenerational dilemma, there is the "consent dilemma." The consent dilemma, according to Kristen Shrader-Frechette, is "that siting radwaste facilities and employing waste management workers requires the consent of those put at risk; yet those most able to give free, informed consent are usually unwilling to do so, and those least able to validly consent are often willing to give alleged consent" (Kristen Shrader-Frechette, "Ethical Dilemmas and Radioactive Waste: A Survey of the Issues," *Environmental Ethics*, 13, 4 (1991):335–339). Those local communities which have lower incomes, no job security, and lower levels of education are more willing to accept the waste. One scholar identifies the problem of siting hazardous wastes in or near rural communities as "environmental racism." Shrader-Frechette argues that the exchange— wages for a job—is grounded in a coercive context which jeopardizes legitimate, free, and informed consent.

6. The proposed Millstone site is near the southern Connecticut shore and has been accepted by the local community. This site was not on the compact's list of potential sites.

7. In addition to *New York v. United States*, the Supreme Court has recently interpreted the commerce clause in such a way that prohibits state and local governments from treating out-of-state hazardous waste differently than local waste. In *Fort Gratiot Sanitary Landfill, Inc. v. Michigan Department of Natural Resources*, No. 91–636, the Court opposed a Michigan law which prevented an operator of a landfill to accept out-of-state wastes unless permission was granted by the county and the state. Also, in *Chemical Waste Management v. Hunt*, No. 91–471, the Court struck down an Alabama statute which required a $72-per-ton fee on wastes brought in from other states. The Court considers hazardous waste to be an element of commerce, and therefore, tariffs or fees placed on out-of-state waste are deemed unconstitutional. Both of these rulings may eventually have an impact on LLRW compact policy development.

8. The California Health Services Department, the lead agency in the compact, has attempted to find a way to acquire the land from the federal government without the Lands Commission's approval (i.e., an attempt to override a potential veto).

9. An administrative approach *similar* to that adopted by the Northwest Power Planning Council's Fish and Wildlife Program might be a model for LLRW to emulate. The council has adopted an adaptive approach. Myriad interests ranging from Indian tribes, local and state governments, and various other public and private interests are arranged in a format similar to a roundtable. Each interest has a voice in decisionmaking. For more on the adaptive approach, see Kai N. Lee and Jody Lawrence, "Adaptive Management: Learning from the Columbia River Basin Fish and Wildlife Program," *Environmental Law*, 16 (1986):431–460.

REFERENCES

Axelrod, Robert. 1986. An Evolutionary Approach to Norms. *American Political Science Review*, 80:1095–1111.

Beer, Samuel H. 1973. The Modernization of American Federalism. *Publius*, 3, 2 (Fall):49–96.

Bella, David A., Charles D. Mosher, and Stephen N. Calvo. 1988. Establishing Trust: Nuclear Waste Disposal. *Journal of Professional Issues in Engineering*, 114 (January):40–50.

Bowman, Ann O'M. 1985. Hazardous Waste Management: An Emerging Policy Area Within an Emerging Federalism. *Publius*, 15 (Winter):131–144.

Bowman, Ann O'M. and Richard Kearney. 1986. *The Resurgence of the States*. Englewood Cliffs, NJ: Prentice Hall.

Carter, L. J. 1987. *Nuclear Imperative and Public Trust: Dealing with Radioactive Waste*. Washington, DC: Resources for the Future.

Chi, Keon S. 1990. Interstate Cooperation: Resurgence of Multistate Regionalism. *The Journal of State Government*, 63, 3 (July-September):59–63.

Cole, Richard L. and David A. Caputo. 1984. The Public Hearing as an Effective Citizen Participation Mechanism: A Case Study of the General Revenue Sharing Program. *American Political Science Review*, 78:404–416.

Condon, David L. 1990. The Never Ending Story: Low-Level Waste and the Exclusionary Authority of Non-compacting States. *Natural Resources Journal*, 30 (Winter):65–86.

Council of Scientific Affairs. 1989. Low Level Radioactive Wastes. *Journal of the American Medical Association*, 26, 5 (August 4):669–674.

Council of State Governments. 1977. *Interstate Compacts: A Revised Compilation*. Lexington, KY: Council of State Governments.

Crenson, Matthew A. 1987. The Private Stake in Public Goods: Overcoming the Illogicy of Collective Action. *Policy Sciences*, 20:259–276.

Davies, Clarence. 1984. Environmental Institutions and the Reagan Administration. In Norman J. Vig and Michael E. Kraft, eds. *Environmental Policy in the 1980s: Reagan's New Agenda*. Washington, DC: Congressional Quarterly.

Davis, Charles E. and James Lester. 1987. Decentralizing Federal Environmental Policy: A Research Note. *Western Political Quarterly*, 40 (September):555–565.

Derthick, Martha. 1974. *Between State and Nation.* Washington, DC: Brookings
    Institution.
Dryzek, John S. 1987. *Rational Ecology.* New York: Basil Blackwell Inc.
Dunlap, Riley E., and Michael E. Kraft, eds. n.d. *Public Opinion and Nuclear Waste:
    Citizens View Repository Siting.* Durham, NC: Duke University Press (forthcom-
    ing).
Erickson, K. 1990. Toxic Reckoning: Business Faces a New Kind of Fear. *Harvard
    Business Review,* 90, 1 (January/February):118–126.
Fitzgerald, Michael R., Amy Snyder McCabe, and David H. Folz. 1988. Federalism and
    the Environment: The View from the States. *State and Local Government Review,*
    (Fall):98–104.
Furiga, Paul. 1989. Hot Stuff. *Governing,* 3 (November):50–54.
Grad, Frank P. 1963. Federal-State Compact: A New Experiment in Co-Operative
    Federalism. *Columbia Law Review,* 63:825–855.
Hardin, Garrett. 1968. The Tragedy of the Commons. *Science,* 162:1243–1248.
Jordan, E. A., C. F. Nern, and M. J. Barianca. 1984. Low-level Waste Management:
    Creating a Stable System in the United States of America. *Radioactive Waste
    Management.* Proceedings of an international conference. Volume 3, International
    Atomic Energy Agency, Vienna.
Kasperson, R. E. 1983. *Equity Issues in Radioactive Waste Management.* Cambridge,
    MA: Oelgelschlager, Gunn and Hain.
——— . 1991. Social Realities in High-Level Waste Management and Their Policy Implica-
    tions. In *Proceedings of the International High-Level Radioactive Waste Manage-
    ment Conference.* New York: American Society of Civil Engineers.
Kearney, Richard C. 1988. Radioactive Waste Compacts: States Move Ahead. In Thad L.
    Beyle, ed. *State Government: CQ's Guide to Current Issues and Activities 1988–
    89.* Lexington, KY: Council of State Governments.
Kearney, Richard C. and John J. Stucker. 1985. Interstate Compacts and the Management
    of Low Level Radioactive Wastes. *Public Administration Review,* (January/Feb-
    ruary):210–220.
Kraft, Michael E. and Bruce B. Clary. 1991. Citizen Participation and the NIMBY
    Syndrome: Public Response to Radioactive Waste Disposal. *Western Political
    Quarterly,* 44 (June):299–328.
Lester, James P. 1986. New Federalism and Environmental Policy. *Publius,* 16 (Fall):89–
    97.
McGinnis, Michael V. 1992. *Towards an Ecological Perspective in Environmental
    Administration.* Ph.D. Dissertation. University of California, Santa Barbara.
Nice, David C. 1987. State Participation in Interstate Compacts. *Publius* 17, (Spring):69–
    84.
Nuclear News. 1988. Southwest Compact Clears Senate, 31 (December):88–89.
O'Hare, Michael, Lawrence Bacow, and Debra Sanderson. 1983. *Facility Siting and
    Public Opposition.* New York: Van Nostrand Reinhold.
Olson, Mancur. 1965. *The Logic of Collective Action.* Cambridge, MA: Harvard Univer-
    sity Press.
O'Riordan, Timothy. 1977. Environmental Ideologies. *Environment and Planning,* 11,
    1:4.

Paehlke, Robert and Douglas Torgerson, eds. 1990. *Managing Leviathan: Environmental Politics and the Administrative State*. Kenmore, NY: Broadview Press.

Pijawka, K. David and Alvin H. Mushkatel. 1992. Public Opposition to the Siting of the High-Level Nuclear Waste Repository. *Policy Studies Review*, 10, 4:180–194.

Ridgeway, Marian. 1971. *Interstate Compacts: A Question of Federalism*. Carbondale, IL: Southern Illinois University Press.

Riggs, Russell W. 1990. Radioactive Waste Compacts for the Northeastern States. *The Journal of State Government*, 63, 3 (July-September):80–82.

Shrader-Frechette, Kristen. 1991. Ethical Dilemmas and Radioactive Waste: A Survey of the Issues. *Environmental Ethics*, 13, 4 (Winter):335–339.

Smiley, J. L. 1984. Radioactive Waste Management in the United States. *Radioactive Waste Management*. Proceedings of the conference organized by the British Nuclear Energy Society, London, November 27–29.

Weart, S. R. 1988. *Nuclear Fear: A History of Images*. Cambridge, MA: Harvard University Press.

Wilson, James Q. 1974. The Politics of Regulation. In James W. McKie, ed. *Social Responsibility and the Business Predicament*. Washington, DC: Brookings Institution.

4

Legal Issues Surrounding Nuclear Waste Storage and Transportation

J. HOLMES ARMSTEAD, JR., *and* KARLEN J. REED

Potential legal liabilities involving toxic substances are among the primary concerns planners must address when developing transportation systems and storage sites for both toxic and nuclear wastes. Fulfillment of legal requirements is only part of the solution. Planners must also anticipate from where legal challenges might come and what the potential outcomes might be. To develop such a long-range view with some reasonable degree of accuracy is a difficult responsibility. Some tools of law can be used to greatly improve the process beyond the guessing stage and provide a measure of comfort and assurance to the planner that the contemplated project will not fail on legal grounds.

There are generally two bodies of law with which a planner must be concerned when developing disposal transportation systems for hazardous materials: (1) the federal, state, and local regulating codes that cover the particular substances with which the project deals, and (2) traditional torts liability theories, including negligence, *res ipsa loquitur*, and strict liability. The regulatory scheme, particularly involving federally mandated requirements for transportation, is covered elsewhere in this text.

This chapter will deal with tort law as it generally applies to the industrial processes, land use planning, and transportation of nuclear waste. The purpose of this chapter is to provide an overview of the general regulatory scheme for nuclear waste as it has grown out of tort law. The authors warn the reader that each state and local government may, and usually does, have peculiar regulatory requirements that reflect local concerns or some unique history. These conditions often give rise to special regulations that may not fit the general scheme that a planner has experienced elsewhere. In either case, local legal counsel with subject matter expertise should be consulted as a part of the planning process from the early stages of project inception so as not to run afoul of unique regulatory requirements or to violate tort law.

FORMULA FOR A TORT

Please excuse the authors' temerity in defining some very basic legal terms and legal concepts discussed in this section on torts. The intended reader is the site developer or systems planner who lacks extensive background in legal analysis and probably does not want detailed information. This first section on torts is designed to provide warning signs so that the reader knows when and where legal trouble may appear and how to act with prudent regard in discussing those concerns with legal counsel before proceeding. The needs of a planner are to know the general legal subject matter involved in a problem, to seek appropriate legal counsel, and to make relevant inquiries that will get the best available information in a timely fashion.

Torts—what are they and why do you need to know about them? So that we may proceed without any unnecessary terminological inexactitude, let us begin by defining torts as they affect the physical planning process. A tort is a civil, not a criminal, wrong that arises outside of a contract. A tort is also an invasion of a private right recognized by law. These are definitions coined by Professor William Prosser and other legal scholars to whom lawyers have deferred over the years.[1] During centuries of its development, the common law, as defined by judges hearing cases, has refined the requirements of personal behavior and conduct whereby its breach has legal consequences, called liability. Courts will award damages[2] or order the restraint of conduct[3] where the defendant[4] is adjudged to have acted tortiously against a plaintiff, that is, the defendant is liable because of his or her action or inaction toward the plaintiff.

Now, let us devise a formula or test for how this liability may attach. This will consequently provide both an early warning to developing problems and an aid in predicting a successful defense where your intended course of action may later be challenged. The first things you need to know are the standards of behavior and how to find out the applicable rules. Court case law provides a general formula that will define tortious conduct and provide a basis for legal analysis for an intended course of action. For any tort to exist, we must have a *prima facie* (foundational) test. All elements of this test must be present to hold the defendant legally liable for his or her conduct. The general elements of the *prima facie* test for the tort of negligence are:

1. Duty owed to the plaintiff.
2. Breach of duty by the defendant.
3. Injury or loss to the plaintiff.
4. Defendant's breach of duty is the proximate cause of plaintiff's injury.

Duty

Duty is the primary *prima facie* element. A person's duty to another is the "duty to use reasonable care."[5] The systems planner must clearly understand this element because the duties involved should be considered at every phase of operational plans. The concept of duty in tort law has ancient origins and can require quite complex analyses in particular applications, as was done by U.S. Supreme Court Justice Benjamin Cardozo in the now famous products liability case of *MacPherson v. Buick Motor Co.*[6]

Inherent in this duty is the concept of foreseeability, a legal fiction of what the ordinary, reasonably prudent person would do in similar circumstances. The law asks whether a danger to the plaintiff was reasonably foreseeable in attempting to fix a duty (and hence liability) upon a defendant.[7] A judgment evaluation is actually part of the definition of foreseeability. Reasonable prudence is a sliding scale test. The prudent engineer or transportation systems planner will have knowledge about toxic waste shipping or nuclear waste storage site construction not within the purview of the average citizen. The law will require the planner to use this "expert" knowledge in protecting the public from the consequences of any "unreasonable risk" taken in implementing a system which exposes the public to danger.

This does not mean we cannot build complex systems which have *some* danger of failure. The duty standard was restated by Justice Cardozo as: "[b]ecause the danger is foreseen there is a duty to avoid the injury."[8] The reasonably prudent planner or systems engineer charged with developing facilities to contain dangerous substances would be held liable for not avoiding foreseeable injury. The extent of injury, should a nuclear release occur in transit or a leak into an aquifer develop, would be so enormous that prudence requires extensive safety measures be taken to reduce that risk to an acceptable level. This has again been phrased by a court in a landmark decision: "The risk reasonably to be perceived defines the duty to be obeyed, and risk imports relation; it is risk to another or to others within the range of apprehension."[9]

Breach of Duty

The duty, of course, defines its breach as failing to do that which by law is required or is prohibited. Observing professional standards of practice will usually protect the conduct from legal challenge. Obviously, the success of programs properly transporting and storing materials without untoward incident is rather unlikely to give rise to any serious legal attack based in torts.

Redundancy is quite useful in insuring a successful storage or transportation program. Should radioactive or toxic materials escape from a primary containment vessel, secondary and tertiary systems which frustrate or prevent nuclear toxic material from contaminating the environment will aid programs' success as well as reduce or eliminate any legal risks. The use of systems that have long histories of success and are subject to repeated testing will also demonstrate prudence.

Damages

Damages must be based on injury to the plaintiff and are a matter of proof. The plaintiff must give evidence of injury in order to recover monetary damages. Injuries arising from negligence in handling nuclear materials may be enormous. Large land masses and groundwater systems can be affected permanently by the release of minute amounts of hazardous materials. The prudent planner must consider whether affected areas would be populated in planning transportation routes or storage sites because the risk of human injury is significant.

A casual review of damages would include the cost of cleaning up the hazardous materials, depreciation of the land's value, the commercial value of facilities lost or denied to owners, destruction of livestock, loss of use of surface and groundwater, displacement costs for personal and business relocation, and most important, physical harm to people affected by an accidental release. Potential damages are a risk assessment measure that is as valuable for fiscal planning as it is for legal planning and should be discussed with legal counsel in the early stages of route or site planning studies. This may very well be the deciding factor as to whether a specific transportation route or facility site is chosen. Incidents are unlikely to occur in a well-planned system. If they are going to occur, the physical placement of routes and sites may be invaluable for gaining clean-up time or providing a distance cushion from any major population centers.

Proximate Cause

Proximate cause is the final link that must connect the defendant's wrongdoing to the plaintiff's injuries. Proximate cause exists where, but for the defendant's action or inaction, the plaintiff would not have suffered the injury for which the action (case) is brought. The proximate or legal cause connects the defendant's action and the plaintiff's injury without intervention by another cause.

These elements can be easily understood by a hypothetical. For example, Ajax Construction receives a contract from the U.S. Department of Energy (DOE) to build a transport containment vessel (TCV) for use in transhipment of nuclear waste materials from various power plant sites to a waste storage facility. The Ajax engineering department goes to work on designing the TCV. During the design and test phase, one of the junior engineers notices that metal fatigue near the welding points of the TCV does not meet design requirements 32 percent of the time. He notifies his team leader, who shuns those findings as insignificant, and no more is said.

Four years later, one of Ajax's TCVs affixed to the flatbed of a tractor-trailer truck rolls off an embankment on Interstate 70. The vessel's integrity is breached, spilling fifteen tons of radioactive liquid wastes. A local stream fed by road ditch runoff water is contaminated with radioactive beryllium, strontium 90, and other unknown contaminants found in the radioactive waste. Upon investigation, the U.S. Environmental Protection Agency (EPA) discovers that progressive metal fatigue near two welds contributed to the vessel's rupture.

Here is the legal analysis that a planner is expected to have undergone when planning transportation routes. Ajax was on notice that there might have been a design flaw. Given their expert knowledge in building a containment vessel for a very dangerous substance, there was a duty to investigate the finding of the young engineer and take proper corrective action. That such an accident could occur with the ensuing rupture was certainly foreseeable by prudent risk analysis. Hence, Ajax will be liable for damages to the nearby landowners and to those injured by groundwater and surface water contamination.

While this was a relatively simplistic scenario, one can estimate the potential liabilities inherent in transporting nuclear waste containment vessels. In this manner the enormous risks of railway and motor vehicle movement could be significantly reduced. The systems planner must also consider the possibilities for problems when large groups of people become involved in developing technologically complex systems that use dangerous materials. Standards of care will be high and varied.

Two other doctrines, *res ipsa loquitur* and strict liability, are worth mentioning. *Res ipsa loquitur* is a legal doctrine applied where a dangerous instrumentality or substance is under the sole control of a defendant and where the instrumentality is not normally subject to escape when prudently handled. Unexplained harm to the plaintiff will bring liability upon the defendant in this case under *res ipsa loquitur*. The second doctrine, strict liability, is closely related and is usually applied by the courts to common carriers and those engaging in extremely dangerous or ultra-hazardous activity such as handling explosives or mining, and so on. If the acts of the defendant are shown to have caused the plaintiff's injury, then liability will follow even though no wrongful quality attaches to the nature of such act. These two theories have been applied to real-life factual situations in a number of significant court cases, as discussed in the next section.

TORT LIABILITY

This section addresses the question: If an accidental release occurs during the transportation or storage of nuclear materials, will the producer, transportation company, or storage company be held responsible for injuries? To answer this question, we must look at tort law liabilities and remedies in light of federal law and court cases that interpret that law.

Congress treats liability for releases and leakages of radioactive materials differently from other types of liability because Congress intended to develop the nuclear industry as a viable source of energy by giving nuclear energy companies special financial incentives. This section will assimilate and integrate basic legal theories with major statutes and case law into a cohesive, understandable framework. The framework is intended to guide the reader in assessing the overall liability issues in transporting and storing radioactive materials.

Tort Theories

As noted, our judicial system imposes liability for injuries caused by torts under various legal theories such as negligence, strict liability, and *res ipsa loquitur*. An example of a tort is injury caused by improperly designed storage units for radioactive materials.

A person injured by a tort can recover damages, which include actual (general and special) damages and, for malicious conduct, punitive damages. Actual damages consist of general and special damages. General damages are the usual and necessary result of the wrongful act, such as lost wages and medical bills. Special damages are those which can be expected, but are not necessarily a result of the wrongful act, such as reimbursement for repossession of a vehicle for lack of wages. Punitive damages are designed to punish the offending party and are usually set at the judge's or jury's discretion, though some jurisdictions base punitive damages on the amount of actual damages awarded.

Damages may be recovered under one or more tort theories so long as the tort theory is not pre-empted, or nullified, by a federal law. State tort laws that conflict with federal laws are pre-empted under the Supremacy Clause of Article VI, clause 2 of the U.S. Constitution.

The U.S. Supreme Court has ruled that state tort remedies, including punitive damages, could be assessed against certain types of companies for radiological injuries, as was done in *Silkwood v. Kerr-McGee Corp.*[10] This case, based on facts underlying a film of the same name, is one of the leading cases on tort liability for injuries from radioactive materials. *Silkwood* established a two-tier test for determining whether a state law was pre-empted by a federal law: (1) whether there is an irreconcilable conflict between the federal and state laws, or (2) whether following a state law in a tort lawsuit would frustrate the objectives of the federal law.[11]

Negligence Theory. Torts come in all shapes and sizes. Most torts are based on the negligence theory. Negligence is the failure to use that amount of care that a reasonable, prudent person would use in the same circumstances. A negligent act is one that does not meet the standard of care that society imposes.

One example of a negligent act is rear-ending the vehicle in front of you when you are not paying attention to your driving. If your negligent act causes injury to the driver ahead of you, then you could be held responsible for that driver's injuries. Another example involves the design of a receptacle meant to store radioactive wastes for 10,000 years. If the receptacle should have been created out of different materials and you negligently designed the receptacle, you could be held liable for all injuries caused by the poor design.

Negligence is one theory often used by the courts to hold an individual or common carrier responsible for injuries arising out of handling nuclear materials. A common carrier is any form of transportation for hire, including taxi cabs, buses, airplanes, trains, and commercial trucking companies. The standard of care for negligence is greater for a common carrier than for the ordinary person because the carrier makes its living by transporting people and commodities.

Strict Liability Theory. The strict liability theory imposes fault if the individual has and fails to perform an absolute duty to make something safe, which causes injuries. Failing to properly label a hazardous substance is an act for which strict liability can be imposed. Strict liability is imposed if the activity is ultra-hazardous or abnormally dangerous. An ultra-hazardous activity, according to *Rylands v. Fletcher*,[12] is an uncommon usage of the land where the landowner cannot eliminate risk by using reasonable care.[13] The U.S. Supreme Court, in *Rylands*, held a landowner liable for damages caused to a downhill mine when his water escaped from an impoundment. Recently, the Washington State Supreme Court, in *Siegler v. Kuhlman*,[14] ruled that common carriers engaged in ultra-hazardous activities could be held liable under a strict liability theory.

An abnormally dangerous activity is similar to an ultra-hazardous activity. A court must consider six factors in determining whether an activity is abnormally dangerous: (1) existence of a high degree of risk of some harm to a person or his or her property, (2) likelihood that there will be great harm, (3) ability to eliminate the risk by using reasonable care, (4) extent to which the activity is not common, (5) inappropriateness of the activity to the place where it is carried on, and (6) extent to which its dangerous attributes outweigh its value to the community.[15] Typical examples of ultra-hazardous activities include blasting, excavation, and operating a nuclear plant.

Res Ipsa Loquitur Doctrine. Related to the negligence theory is the *res ipsa loquitur* doctrine. Under this doctrine, an injured party that cannot identify which of several defendants is responsible for the injury can assert negligence against all the defendants if the instrument of injury was within the sole control of the defendants and if the injury was not caused by negligence of the injured party.

The next phase in understanding tort liability for transporting and storing nuclear materials is to briefly review the significant federal laws and court cases that interpret those laws.

SIGNIFICANT LEGISLATION AND CASE LAW

We begin with a brief overview of the major federal legislation that regulates the transportation and storage of radioactive materials.

The Atomic Energy Act of 1954[16] is the primary source of federal authority for regulating nuclear materials. This statute was the basis for the U.S. Supreme Court's ruling that the federal government has the right to regulate control and operation of nuclear materials, including disposal of nuclear wastes.[17] This act was intended to promote the peaceful development and use of nuclear energy.

The Price-Anderson Act,[18] originally passed in 1957, amended the Atomic Energy Act by encouraging financial responsibility of nuclear plant owners. Plant owners who obtained sufficient liability insurance according to this act's guidelines were shielded from unlimited tort recovery and indemnified by the federal government for their losses.

The act was amended in 1966 to prohibit participating nuclear entities from asserting legal defenses of governmental immunity and contributory negligence. Prior to this time, nuclear power plants could claim governmental immunity, that is, protection from lawsuits, because they were licensed by the federal government, which cannot be sued absent specific federal legislation authorizing such suit. Likewise, the power plants could reduce or avoid liability if they could show that the injured person was partly at fault, that is, contributorily negligent. These defenses were waived by the 1966 amendment.

Amendments in 1988[19] limited liability to $560 million in the event of an extraordinary nuclear occurrence. An extraordinary nuclear occurrence is a discharge of nuclear material offsite which the Nuclear Regulatory Commission (NRC) determines will probably result in substantial damages to persons or property offsite.[20]

Under this act, punitive damages cannot be awarded for a nuclear incident or a precautionary evacuation against any entity that has agreed to indemnification provisions of this act.[21] Liability limits on awarding punitive damages do not apply to entities not required by the NRC to maintain financial responsibility under Price-Anderson.[22]

Under *Bennett v. Mallinckrodt, Inc.,*[23] federal laws regulating radiation standards do not forbid use of state tort law remedies, including strict liability, because handling radioactivity is an abnormally dangerous activity. State tort law remedies apply to injuries arising out of nuclear accidents, but the Price-Anderson Act will also apply.[24]

The Price-Anderson Act does not clearly provide the same liability dollar limit protection to transporters and storers of radioactive wastes as it does to nuclear producers. Because of this, most, if not all, companies that transport or store nuclear materials attempt to obtain liability insurance sufficient to cover injuries and damages caused by accidental spills. The inherent high risks make obtaining insurance coverage difficult at a reasonable premium. The standard comprehensive general liability insurance policy used by most businesses does not adequately cover possible hazardous spills.

Many policies specifically exclude damages resulting from the discharge, release, or escape of toxic fumes or chemicals and radioactivity. A special endorsement must be obtained from the insurance agent or broker to cover these types of accidents. Insurance companies will rarely, however, insure against claims for punitive damages, civil fines, and penalties.

These endorsements vary greatly in coverage, so one must closely examine the policy and all endorsements to accurately determine the extent of coverage.

The National Environmental Policy Act of 1969 (NEPA) details the environmental review process. The NRC is required by NEPA to consider environmental consequences at every stage of the decisionmaking process in licensing and operating nuclear plants and disposal operations. Although the NRC is required to consider environmental consequences in its environmental impact statement, only those consequences that are feasible must be studied.

This was most pointedly brought out in the case of *Carolina Environmental Study Group v. United States*,[25] in which the NRC's predecessor, the Atomic Energy Commission (AEC), scaled the probable consequences of reactor accidents from one to nine. Nine was the most severe, meaning a breach of the containment vessel and release of nuclear materials. Because the probability of a Class Nine accident was so low, the U.S. Supreme Court said the AEC was not required to study or discuss the probable effects of such a scenario.[26]

The U.S. Environmental Protection Agency has been charged with enforcing the clean-up provisions of the Comprehensive Environmental Response, Compensation, and Liability Act of 1980 (CERCLA)[27] and its amendments contained in the Superfund Amendment and Reauthorization Act of 1986. Among their other attributes, these statutes require tracing liability for spills and leakages of hazardous materials through the chain of custody, from generator to transporter to storage to disposal. Should a spill of nuclear materials occur during transportation or storage, the EPA and its state counterpart will lead the clean-up, site assessment, and liability assessment under these two acts.

The Nuclear Waste Policy Act of 1982 was passed to resolve how to dispose of high-level radioactive waste within the United States. This act was Congress's compromise to resolve disposal problems surrounding high-level radioactive fuel. A fair, scientific method of finding the best site for a high-level nuclear waste repository was presented. Originally planned were locations for two repositories, coupled with development of a monitored retrievable storage facility for packaging the waste prior to shipment.

This act imposed a 70,000-metric-ton limit as the maximum amount of total high-level radioactive waste that could be stored at the repository. The waste would be contained within 700 bore holes that would hold 24,000 canisters of waste. No mining and no water pumping would be allowed in the underlying aquifer per environmental protection standards.

Under this act, the DOE is required to locate a site that will isolate the radioactive waste from the biosphere for 10,000 years.[28]

The Nuclear Waste Policy Amendments Act of 1987 proposed Yucca Mountain, Nevada, as a high-level nuclear waste repository. The other proposed repository sites were the Hanford Reservation, Washington, and Deaf Smith County, Texas. Plans for the monitored retrieval storage facility were scrapped until the high-level repository is constructed. The act provides that if Yucca Mountain is determined to be unsuitable as a nuclear repository, the DOE must report back to Congress for further instructions or legislation.

Nevada's state nuclear project office is currently spearheading a grassroots effort to discover and expose various ways in which Yucca Mountain is unsuitable for the repository. Earthquakes, potential groundwater contamination, threats from terrorism, military testing at the nearby Nevada Nuclear Test Site, nearby oil and natural gas deposits, and the adverse effects on local tourism are some ways in which Yucca Mountain is alleged to be unsuitable.[29]

The Hazardous Materials Transportation Act[30] (HMTA) was passed to allow safe transportation of hazardous materials, which are defined as materials which may pose an unreasonable risk to health and safety or property when transported in commerce.[31] State regulations will not be pre-empted if they adopt or do not conflict with the Atomic Energy Act and HMTA.

An example of this occurred in Ohio in *N.Y. State Energy Research & Dev. v. Nuclear Fuel Service, Inc.*[32] Ohio attempted to prohibit transportation of nuclear waste across its state borders, but the federal court held that state statutes were pre-empted because the NRC had exclusive jurisdiction over transporting nuclear wastes. Similar results came from the state of Washington in *Washington State Bldg. & Constr. Trades Council v. Spellman.*[33]

The Federal Tort Claims Act[34] provides the exclusive remedy for tort claims against the United States that arise out of nondiscretionary acts, defined in 28 U.S.C. §2680 (a). This has been a useful vehicle in recovering damages on a tort claim arising out of exposure to radiation drifting from the Nevada Nuclear Test Site.[35] The Utah federal district court, in another suit concerning the Nevada Nuclear Test Site, held that the two-year time limitation in which plaintiffs could sue could not be applied wholesale to an entire group of plaintiffs.[36]

Bennett v. Mallinckrodt, Inc.[37] allowed the plaintiffs to seek medically verified damages for emotional distress and physical injuries caused by radioactive isotopes that escaped from a neighboring radiopharmaceutical processing plant. Probable damages estimated by means of mathematical probabilities are not considered medically verified. This case also holds that a nuclear incident can occur over an extended period of time, such as occurs in prolonged exposure to leaking radioactive materials from an undetected site.

CONCLUSION

The answer to the question posed earlier in this chapter, whether liability can be imposed on nuclear waste disposal carriers and producers under certain tort theories in certain circumstances, is a qualified "yes." Three tort theories—negligence, strict liability for abnormally dangerous activities, and *res ipsa loquitur*—can be used to recover damages for a plaintiff's injuries.

Congress has passed special legislation that affords some protection to nuclear generators that are willing to participate in programs set up by the Price-Anderson Act. Tort liability limits do not apply where the generator does not participate. State tort law remedies that do not conflict with federal law can be used to recover damages for injuries from radioactive materials. Two recent pieces of legislation, the Nuclear Waste Policy Act of 1982 and the Nuclear Waste Policy Amendments Act of 1987, will place states, particularly Nevada, in the position of making sure their citizens receive the fullest amount of tort protection allowed.

Public fears of nuclear releases can, as discussed in other chapters in this text, force public planners to require stringent regulations on those who store and transport nuclear wastes. Failure to follow those regulations can result in serious liabilities and financial consequences. The planning design and construction phases of a repository program should therefore adhere to basic principles of tort law regarding liability.

NOTES

1. Prosser, *The Law of Torts*, 7th ed., New York: Gilbert Foundation Press, 1982. This volume and its predecessors have been subjected to such wide use in U.S. law schools in the past four decades as to give rise to an often quoted if somewhat trite jibe that "Prosser on Torts is like sterling on silver."

2. Damages are the extent to which the courts recognize harm to the injured party and are usually expressed in a money judgment being awarded at the conclusion of a case.

3. Where money damages under the legal rules are insufficient to compensate a plaintiff for injury suffered and/or where that injury is the subject of continuing conduct on the part of the defendant, the rules of equity may be invoked by a court in fashioning an appropriate remedy. A defendant may be enjoined (prohibited) from a particular course of conduct deemed wrongfully injurious to the plaintiff.

4. The courts usually decide cases based upon the common law rule of *stare decisis*, that is, where a principle has been decided by a court, that decision shall stand as a rule or precedent to be followed by later courts of the same jurisdiction when considering the same issue. This system is generally felt to promote justice by providing order and predictability to the litigation process. This is the very cornerstone of the common law or more correctly the "case law" system we follow in the United States.

5. 28 *Columbia Law Review* at p. 1025.

6. *MacPherson v. Buick Motor Co.*, 217 N.Y. 382, 111 N.E. 1050 (1916).

7. *Cobb vs. Twitchell*, 91 Fla. 539, 108 So. 186 (1926).

8. *Glanzer vs. Shepard*, 233 N.Y. 236, 135 N.E. 275 (1922).

9. *Palsgraf vs. Long Island R.R.*, 162 N.E. 99 (1928).

10. *Silkwood v. Kerr-McGee Corp.*, 667 F.2d 908, (10th Cir. 1981), *reversed on other grounds* 464 U.S. 238, 78 L.Ed.2d 443, 104 S.Ct. 615 (1984), *rehearing denied* 465 U.S. 1074, 79 L.Ed.2d 754, 104 S.Ct. 1430, *on remand* 769 F.2d 1451 (10th Cir.), *cert. denied* 476 U.S. 1104, 90 L.Ed.2d 356, 106 S.Ct. 1947. The jury awarded Ms. Silkwood's estate $500,000 for personal injuries, $5,000 for property damage, and $10 million for punitive damages. *Silkwood*, 104 S.Ct. at 619.

11. *Silkwood*, 104 S.Ct. at 626.

12. *Rylands v. Fletcher*, 3 H.L. 330 (1868).

13. Restatement (First) Torts, §520.

14. *Siegler v. Kuhlman*, 81 Wash.2d 448, 502 P.2d 1181 (1972), *cert. denied* 411 U.S. 983, 36 L.Ed.2d 959, 93 S.Ct. 2275 (1973).

15. Restatement (Second) Torts, §520 (1977).

16. 42 U.S.C. §§2011–2282.

17. *Northern States Power Co. v. Minnesota*, 447 F.2d 1143 (8th Cir. 1971), *affirmed* 405 U.S. 1035 (1972); *Pacific Gas & Electric Co. v. State Energy Resources Conservation & Development Commission*, 461 U.S. 190 (1983).

18. 42 U.S.C. §2210.

19. Public Law 100–408.

20. 42 U.S.C. §2014(j) .

21. 42 U.S.C. §2210(s). The U.S. Supreme Court ruled that the liability dollar limits set by the Price-Anderson Act did not violate either the Equal Protection or the Due Process clauses of the Fifth Amendment to the U.S. Constitution because the act was intended to promote financial responsibility among nuclear waste producers. *Duke Power Co. v. Carolina Environmental Study Group, Inc.*, 438 U.S. 59, 57 L.Ed.2d 595, 98 S.Ct. 2620 (1978).

22. *Silkwood*, 104 S.Ct. at 623.

23. *Bennett v. Mallinckrodt, Inc.*, 698 S.W.2d 854, *cert. denied* 476 U.S. 1176, 90 L.Ed.2d 989, 106 S.Ct. 2903 (1985).

24. *Kiick v. Metropolitan Edison Co.*, 784 F.2d 490 (3rd Cir. 1986).

25. *Carolina Environmental Study Group v. United States*, 510 F.2d 796 (D.C. Cir. 1975).

26. This decision was handed down before the March 28, 1979, Three Mile Island Class Nine meltdown and the April 26, 1986, Chernobyl Class Nine meltdown. Despite these disasters, the probability of a Class Nine meltdown still is not required in an environmental impact statement. This court ruling may be subject to reconsideration in light of the proliferation of nuclear power sites constructed since the Three Mile Island and Chernobyl incidents.

27. 42 U.S.C. §§9601–9657.

28. Nevada Nuclear Waste Factsheets 2 and 4, page 1, March 1988, published by the Nevada Nuclear Waste Project Office, Carson City, Nevada.

29. Id.

30. 49 U.S.C. §§1801 et seq.

31. 49 U.S.C. §1802(2).

32. *N.Y. State Energy Research & Dev. v. Nuclear Fuel Service, Inc.*, 102 FRD 18 (W.D. NY 1983).

33. *Washington State Bldg. & Constr. Trades Council v. Spellman*, 518 F.Supp. 928 (E.D. Wash. 1981), *affirmed on other grounds* 684 F.2d 627, *cert. denied* 461 U.S. 913, 77 L.Ed.2d 282, 103 S.Ct. 1981.

34. 28 U.S.C. §§1346, and 2671 et seq.

35. *Prescott v. United States*, 523 F.Supp 918 (D.C. Nev. 1981).

36. *Allen v. United States*, 527 F.Supp. 476 (D.C. Utah 1981), *later proceeding* 588 F.Supp. 247, *reversed on other grounds* 816 F.2d 1417 (10th Cir.). *cert. denied* 484 U.S. 1004, 98 L.Ed.2d 647, 108 S.Ct. 694.

37. *Bennett v. Mallinckrodt, Inc.*, 698 S.W.2d 854, *cert. denied* 476 U.S. 1176, 90 L.Ed.2d 989, 106 S.Ct. 2903 (1985).

5

Critical Organization and Management Issues in Nuclear Waste Disposal

BRIAN COOK

In an article that is now a required citation for anyone writing on nuclear power and radioactive waste, Alvin Weinberg (1972) argued that the choice to pursue nuclear power placed two fundamental demands on U.S. society. First, it required the exercise of the very best techniques in nuclear technology and the use of personnel of paramount expertise and purpose. Second, it required longevity in social institutions. The choice to use nuclear energy, in other words, implied a commitment to a permanent social order with particular institutional arrangements. With respect to nuclear weapons, Weinberg noted, this meant the emergence of a "military priesthood" responsible for deployment, maintenance, and strategic doctrine.

With the penetration of nuclear energy into the fabric of social life, in the generation of electricity, medical diagnostics, and industrial processes, the clear meaning for social structure has yet to emerge. It might mean, Weinberg speculated, the creation of "nuclear parks"—places on the earth where radioactive operations would be continued in perpetuity. Hence they would become permanent features of civilization. This in turn implied that the social apparatus for dealing with radioactive wastes indefinitely would be in place.

As Weinberg noted, the challenge posed by radioactive waste was particularly daunting because few if any human institutions, let alone modern public or private bureaucracies, have endured as long as the time span over which spent nuclear fuel, high-level waste, and even some low-level waste will remain dangerous to human populations and ecosystems. To students of public administration, this very well might be the ultimate challenge to organizational design and managerial strategy. However, formal organizational monitoring and control did not much enter into the long-range planning for radioactive waste disposal through the 1970s and 1980s. Instead, planners and policymakers chose to consider seriously only various "maintenance-free" devices—interpretable markers on the surface at disposal sites, long-lived records, and alternative social institutions—as solutions for how to inform generations to come of the dubious gift left to them.

Unfortunately, the initial disinclination to employ formal organizations in any long-term solution to the radioactive waste problem introduced a bias into policymaking and implementation, including decisions about support for research unfavorable to the considered study and treatment of organization and management issues. This is not to say that policymakers have completely neglected the problems of organization and management for radioactive waste disposal. The flurry of government-funded analyses of the institutional and organizational arrangements that would best support implementation of national policy for high-level waste disposal sponsored between 1977 and 1984 suggests otherwise. With the exceptions of Daniel Metlay (1978), Randall Smith (1980), and Jackie Burns (1981), however, these analyses have focused on general institutional restructuring, in particular, placing implementation into the hands of a quasi-public or private entity instead of a public agency (Willrich and Lester, 1977; U.S. DOE, 1979; Braitman, 1983; U.S. DOE, 1984; U.S. OTA, 1985).[1] The assumption among planners, policymakers, and researchers seems to have been, as is usually the case with policy implementation and administration (Derthick, 1990), that the "details" of organization and management could be left to public or private managers and executives, and thus need not be considered in initial policy design.[2]

It should not come as a complete surprise that many of these details have begun to emerge as obstacles to success for public policy toward radioactive waste. In this chapter, I discuss three organization and management issues that have not received sufficient attention from scholars or policymakers concerned with the problem of radioactive waste. I have intentionally oriented the discussion toward the immediate and longer-run future, rather than dwelling on the mistakes of the past. I have also selected what I consider more comprehensive issues. Others of narrower scope, such as transportation and the conduct of science, are addressed to some extent in other chapters in this volume. My fundamental argument is that because these issues are far-reaching, they pose significant challenges to policy success. Hence they require sustained scrutiny not just by public managers, but by scholars, elected officials, and other interested parties if progress is to made in policy development for radioactive waste.

ORGANIZATIONAL MAINTENANCE

Can formal organizations, particularly public agencies, be given responsibility for monitoring and control of a radioactive waste repository over the long, long time frames during which the wastes will remain dangerous to public health and the environment? The question may sound absurd on its face because the sheer time span, as long as 10,000 years, would seem to prohibit planned organizational monitoring and control. With even a substantially lower time horizon, however, a major organizational maintenance problem exists because the most active stages of a radioactive waste disposal project, including siting, design, construction, operations, closure, and early postclosure monitoring, may span 100 years or more. During that time, a dedicated formal organization must oversee those stages. It thus must be maintained.

As James Q. Wilson (1989) has stressed, organizational maintenance means not only survival but also prosperity. Organizational prosperity in turn requires autonomy and resources. Neither of these is easy for a public organization to achieve and maintain in a liberal democratic regime, and failure to achieve and maintain them means a constant threat to survival as well. In the United States, the relatively focused effort to develop a geologic repository for spent fuel and high-level waste from commercial nuclear power is into its third decade, and the original organization responsible, and its immediate successor, have already met their demise and have been partially reincarnated in a third agency. Calls for yet another organizational restructuring persist.

Much of the source of the problem lies with basic political and governmental structures. Public organizations and the executives that lead them control the degree of autonomy and the flow of resources they enjoy to only a very limited extent. Numerous and varied entities external to the organization have numerous and varied things to say about the autonomy and resources an organization will command, and they have differential authority and power to back up what they say. Thus the autonomy and resources at the disposal of an organization are always contingent and nothing is ever settled (Wilson, 1989:197). Because radioactive waste management is a collective problem posing substantial public health, environmental, economic, social equity, and constitutional questions, moreover, it is difficult to imagine that the form of the responsible organization, whether public, quasi-public, or private, will make much difference in the extent to which outside entities will impose limits on its autonomy and on the resources at its disposal.[3]

What then can be said about the possibility of successful organizational maintenance for radioactive waste management agencies? Acquiring and maintaining stable constituency support is one key. One way to do this is to link the work of the organization with a professional specialty, as in forestry and the U.S. Forest Service, or antitrust law and the Federal Trade Commission. One can similarly envision the development of a radioactive waste management profession linked to the work of waste management organizations. This would be in keeping with Weinberg's call for personnel of high expertise and purpose, and is something akin to the notion of a nuclear priesthood.

The effort would face major obstacles, of course. For example, radioactive waste management requires knowledge and expertise across the physical sciences, engineering, and the social sciences that would be difficult to distill into a single professional paradigm. In addition, organizations closely tied to particular professions are subject to shifting intellectual currents within the profession that can radically alter the mission of the organization from within (e.g., Eisner, 1991).

More than establishing an external constituency that can help to sustain the organization, the organization's own leadership may be most critical to its maintenance. As Wilson (1989:217) argues, "The greatest executives infuse their organizations with value and convince others that this value is not merely useful to the bureau but essential to the polity." Can leaders of radioactive waste management organizations accomplish such a feat? The prospects appear slim because the threat radioactive waste poses is not very pleasant to contemplate. Once the wastes are safely buried away, why would the nation want to maintain the most visible reminders of that threat—the organizations that supervised the disposal?[4]

The radioactive waste management enterprise thus may contain a self-limiting factor with respect to leadership. No one interested in building a public or private organization into an essential component of the regime would take the job since the organization is expected to expire after a century anyway. Moreover, even "great executives" do not live or serve forever. More than one or two generations of exceptional leaders would have to be coaxed into supervising the organization during the most active stages of the waste disposal project.

Of course, constituency building, leadership, and other attributes that may be associated with organizational maintenance may prove to be tangential to sustaining radioactive waste management organizations for sufficient lengths of time. As Herbert Kaufman (1991) has recently hypothesized, chance may be the single most important influence on which organizations survive and prosper, and which expire. Even Wilson

(1989:217) acknowledges that executives with exceptional talents must rely in part on "their good fortune in holding office at a time when their political environment is unusually malleable."

Kaufman's hypothesis is a call for new and varied research on organizational maintenance and evolution. If policymakers, the nuclear industry, and the public would prefer to rely on more than luck for the success of the waste management enterprise, support for research specifically on organizational maintenance in radioactive waste management is necessary. To bring the discussion of organizational maintenance full circle, what that research might very well reveal is that organizational maintenance is more an external than an internal matter. In other words, the varied and conflicting interests involved in radioactive waste policy development will have to make the kinds of commitments and agreements necessary to sustain the organization (giving it adequate autonomy and resources) over the 100-year active life of the waste disposal project. Success in policy formulation on those terms is the first step toward success in policy implementation.

STABILITY, PERFECTION, AND FLEXIBILITY

In recent commentary on the nation's high-level radioactive waste program, the National Research Council's Board on Radioactive Waste Management recommended that the Nuclear Regulatory Commission (NRC) reconsider its detailed licensing requirements for a high-level waste repository. The board argued that the current NRC approach is based on the model of nuclear power plant licensing, and shaped by U.S. administrative law and "a governmental structure that disperses authority among legislative and executive agencies and separates regulation from implementation" (NRC, 1990:25).

The power plant licensing model is inappropriate for the siting, design, construction, and operation of a geologic repository, the board contended, because the properties of geologic media cannot be determined and specified in advance to a degree analogous to that required for man-made components, such as the reinforcing rods, structural concrete, and pipes of a nuclear power plant. The long time frames over which even the man-made components of the repository must remain intact make their performance more difficult to determine than the components of a nuclear power plant with a thirty- or even sixty-year life span. Hence the board concludes that repository development must be more "qualitative." Surprises encountered along the way must be incorporated with past experience and used to modify models, plans, and designs. In short, a flexible, even experimental approach must supplant a rigidly specified approach (also see Cook et al., 1990).

The alteration in organization and management urged by the board reflects the mature scientific and technical consensus about the fundamental character of the radioactive waste disposal enterprise. But the nature of the problem, as reflected in the board's assessment, poses two distinct dilemmas for both high-level and low-level radioactive waste management organizations. These dilemmas have yet to be adequately appreciated by policymakers or their advisors like the board.

The first of these dilemmas is, in many respects, an external, organizational maintenance problem, which only adds to the problematic character of this challenge to radioactive waste policy success. The external demands that executives of radioactive waste management organizations must grapple with, and which appear to be forcing them to structure and operate their organizations contrary to what the science and technology of the waste problem require, do not merely stem from the basics of administrative law and governmental structure as understood by the board. The demands derive from a complex combination of basic features of the U.S. liberal-democratic regime, major regime transformations in the twentieth century that have included changes in public philosophy about the nature and purpose of government, and public perceptions of risk that are themselves closely intertwined with changes in public philosophy.

As a substantial body of research now argues, conclusions about the irrationality of public perceptions of risk—for example, that people think little about engaging in the highly risky activity of driving an automobile while agonizing over a relatively risk-free activity such as living near a nuclear power plant—are misleading (e.g., Slovic et al., 1991). The public's risk calculus has a distinctive logic to it, based in part on whether a risk is borne voluntarily or involuntarily, and on the catastrophic potential of even very low-risk activities. These dimensions of public risk perception shape and are shaped by currently dominant views about the nature and purpose of government.

The extensive reform movement of the late 1960s and early 1970s fostered a "rights revolution" (Sunstein, 1990), in which the definition of rights was expanded beyond the enumerated political rights of the Constitution and the economic security rights of the New Deal to encompass quality-of-life issues such as environmental clean-up, and workplace health and safety. Concomitant with the redefinition of rights was a reinterpretation of the nature and purpose of government. No longer was government only to protect private property and personal liberties, and guarantee economic security; it must now provide a more-than-minimal level of quality of life by managing risks, particularly through regulation. The nation remains a liberal democracy, however, so that a distinction between a public and a private sphere is still appropriate. Activities that pose even a high probability of harm, if engaged in voluntarily, remain a matter of private choice, and little governmental interference is tolerated. Risks faced involuntarily, stemming from nature, from societal processes, or from the actions of government, particularly if they carry a high potential for catastrophe even though the probability of occurrence is minuscule, belong in the province of the public sector. It is government's responsibility, again through regulation and other means, to reduce to a minimum the public's exposure to such risks.

A substantial number of issues dwell in a gray area between the two extremes of private and public risks, and they tend to be quite controversial. Radioactive waste management clearly falls into the public risk category, however. Radioactive waste management organizations thus face external demands that the risks of long-term storage and disposal be reduced to the lowest possible level, and that proof of the ability of the organization to meet and maintain this minimal level of risk be provided *before* any substantial waste management activities, such as repository site investigations, are undertaken. Again, regulatory proceedings provide the principal means for establishing such proof.[5]

Executives of radioactive waste management organizations thus face a seemingly inescapable dilemma. Choosing a more qualitative, flexible, even experimental approach will not neutralize external demands for prior proof of risk reduction and error minimization, and may undermine the fragile public support for and trust in the organization and its mission (Easterling, 1992). Choosing the rigidly specified approach threatens to drag out the waste disposal enterprise indefinitely or derail it completely as surprises crop up that have not been anticipated in regulations, plans, and designs.

One potentially fruitful path of escape from this dilemma lies in the development of a sophisticated risk communications system. Indeed, in its recommendations the Radioactive Waste Management Board urges the Department of Energy (DOE) to undertake "greatly expanded risk communication efforts, aimed at reaching appropriate and achievable goals acceptable to the U.S. public" (NRC, 1990:32). This clearly cannot be a one-way system, in which the DOE or any other waste management organization transmits information about risks to the public largely in an effort to alter or "rationalize" perceptions of public risk. Instead, it must be a two-way system in which the waste management organization communicates with the public about the reducible and irreducible risks associated with radioactive waste disposal, and gathers information about public perceptions of the risks that are then used to develop or modify the design, siting, construction, and operation of a waste facility.[6] To employ such a system effectively, radioactive waste management organizations will require a substantial level of external understanding and support from policymakers and other interested parties.

The requirement for a more qualitative, flexible, contingent strategy poses a second, internal, management dilemma for any radioactive waste management organization. Formal organizations are creatures of stability and routine. They are created to reduce uncertainty and the haphazard response to surprise that leads to error. These basic characteristics will be reinforced in radioactive waste management organizations, as in all public organizations, by organizational maintenance needs. To remain stable and mission-focused for 100 years or so, a waste management organization must maintain strong external support for its resources and authority. It will, therefore, resist changing what it does or how it does it in ways that threaten that external support.

Of course, both private and public organizations operate in environments in constant states of flux. Hence, most formal organizations are constantly changing and adapting, but most of these changes and adaptations are defensive, intended to preserve the core tasks that define an organization's existence. Adopting a flexible, qualitative, contingent strategy amounts to a substantial redefinition of the core tasks of any existing waste management organization. Resistance to such a transformation will be palpable both inside and outside the organization, and it is unclear how that resistance might be overcome.

It is important to recognize that such resistance is not groundless. Being more open, responsive, contingent, and flexible in its operations may lead a waste management organization to adapt first and ask questions later. However, "Innovation is not inevitably good; there are at least as many bad changes as good" (Wilson, 1989:227). Bad changes are likely to persist in public organizations, moreover, because of the absence of a market test for innovations and the intense scrutiny to which public organizations are subject, which make it difficult for executives and managers to admit error and correct mistakes. Would the American public be willing to accept a more open, flexible management approach to radioactive waste disposal and the inevitable errors that would result? The work of Michael Elliott (1984) suggests that they might, if waste management organizations place greater emphasis on accident mitigation and error correction.

Ultimately, the challenge is to find an organizational structure and managerial strategy that strive to minimize error while being prepared to correct the mistakes that will inevitably occur, and that balance the need for stability and mission focus with the need to adapt to new knowledge and perspectives on the problem. The operators, managers, and executives of waste management organizations, as well as policymakers, their advisors, and other external actors must all be involved in the effort, and they will not discover one best way. This means that like the science and technology and the social and economic impacts of waste facility development, organization and management must be the subject of continued research and decisionmaking. That is one of the legacies of choosing to embrace nuclear power.

FROM PUBLIC PARTICIPATION TO PUBLIC CONTROL

My brief references to the necessary conditions for an effective risk communications program and the need for broad involvement in the development of organizational structure and managerial strategy suggest that public participation will be a central issue in the ongoing development of nuclear waste policy. Indeed, demands for the expansion of public participation have been a critical dimension of the politics of nuclear power and radioactive waste since the late 1960s. The failure of the Atomic Energy Commission to respond adequately to such demands played a role in its demise.

Although notable dissent exists, the consensus among scholars and practitioners is that the Nuclear Waste Policy Act of 1982 marked a significant advance in the cause of public participation in nuclear waste policy development through its requirements for consultation and cooperation and the opportunity for states or Indian tribes to veto a site suitability decision, subject to override by both houses of Congress. In the legislative and regulatory developments for low-level waste, however, many states appear to be going beyond substantial arrangements for public participation to provisions for shared public authority and control of waste facilities. The federal government may ultimately be required to follow suit.

In Massachusetts, for example, the law requires that if a low-level waste facility is sited in the state, the membership of the Low-Level Waste Management Board must be expanded to include two representatives of the host community. The law also requires significant site community control over environmental review of the site, and directs the site community, through a Community Supervisory Committee, to select the facility operator, the type of facility to be designed and constructed, and the disposal and containment technology to be employed. The Community Supervisory Committee also has independent inspection and monitoring authority under the law.

Provisions such as these, which require government agencies to share authority over and control of their programs with the public in the form of a legally sanctioned, formally organized public advocate, pose challenges to public organization and management that are unprecedented, save perhaps for the community action programs of the War on Poverty. One worrisome aspect of these provisions is that they authorize a community to stop the development of a facility without the community also bearing any of the responsibility or liability for such a decision. This authorization is analogous to the effective impact of the federal government's bank and savings and loan insurance funds, which served to loosen the fiduciary responsibility of bank and savings and loan officers. Some then behaved recklessly in handling their institutions' funds, to the substantial detriment of the public purse and the public trust. On a smaller scale, might the same result obtain in the development of low-level waste facilities? Can state governments or their agency designates really be held responsible for the actions of independent community supervisory committees?

From an internal perspective, public managers at all levels of government certainly have had considerable experience with sharing control and authority of policy implementation with other agencies and other governmental levels. If local community control essentially means local *government* control, then radioactive waste managers and executives will have a wealth of experience to draw on in implementing provisions like those in Massachusetts law. On the other hand, local community control conceived broadly to include not just local elected and appointed officials but also major organized and unorganized segments of the public in project decisionmaking implies a major advance in the democratization of public administration. Can effective policy implementation and facility management occur in the wake of such an advance?

Again, public managers are not wholly unprepared for the transformation in waste management that shared authority and control might bring about. At least since the emergence of the New Public Administration movement, the push for the democratization of the administrative state has been ongoing, and its effects can be seen in the requirements for citizen participation in federal and state statutes and local ordinances, and in the plentitude of citizen advisory commissions operating at all governmental levels. More generally, the U.S. administrative process is certainly more open and responsive than the corporatist arrangements dominant in Western Europe and Japan. It remains unclear, however, just how broadly public managers and executives conceive the appropriateness of citizen involvement in policy implementation (e.g., Aberbach and Rockman, 1978; Gruber, 1987).

Proponents of further democratizing public administration argue that it would improve not only the democratic process, but the administrative process as well. Some research, including studies of hazardous and nuclear waste facility siting (e.g., Paehlke and Torgerson, 1990), suggests that it might, but the evidence generally from a very limited body of research is mixed. Moreover, the effect of not just open, two-way communications systems and other vehicles for community involvement but of actual shared statutory authority and control has been investigated even less, if at all. One aspect of such extensive public involvement that deserves special attention is the increase in system complexity likely to result from attempts to respond to public concerns in system design and operations. As Charles Perrow (1984) has convincingly argued, the greater the organizational and technical complexity, the greater the chances of system error and, ultimately, catastrophic failure.

Like the radioactive waste management effort as a whole, considerable uncertainty will accompany policy implementation and facility management based on a model of shared authority and control. No amount of anticipatory research and planning will eliminate all the uncertainty. Expanding the base of knowledge seems only prudent in the face of that uncertainty. Policymakers and their advisors can improve the chances of success for what is essentially an experiment in public management by supporting systematic analysis of the potential consequences of shared authority and control, what obstacles might be encountered, including administrator attitudes and receptivity toward public involvement and control, and how the obstacles might be overcome. If policymakers also recognize that radioactive waste management under shared authority and control is itself contingent, qualitative, and not conducive to predetermined models of implementation and organization, they will be positioned to respond intelligently and reasonably when citizens, local officials, or public managers complain that something is not working.

CONCLUSION

Administrative agencies have been at the center of the troubles and controversy engendered by nuclear waste policy, but their organization and management problems have largely been ignored. Although considerable time, money, and effort have been expended in trying to decide if some new organization ought to be placed in charge of the nation's commercial high-level waste program, for example, almost no attention has been directed toward the internal structural, personnel, and strategic problems this organization faces irrespective of its public or private form. These problems are, of course, traditionally the province of the administrator. In casting light upon three particularly demanding challenges radioactive waste managers face, however, I have tried to show not only that organization and management are critical to nuclear waste policy development, but also that broader external learning and attention to the management dimension will enhance the chances of policy success.

NOTES

1. It is important to note that as of Spring 1993, the Secretary of Energy's Advisory Board Task Force on Civilian Radioactive Waste Management is scrutinizing organizational and managerial problems, including a review by the National Academy of Public Administration of "best practices."

2. This seems particularly true of the low-level waste problem, in which the federal government left not only the details of administration but also policy development generally to the states. The states in turn have struggled to give adequate attention to organization and management issues in the low-level waste policies they have developed. Regional compacts created by groups of states to handle low-level waste disposal pose particularly challenging questions about the choice of implementing organizations and management strategies that are beyond the scope of this chapter.

3. One might argue that private entities have an advantage because they can draw on the resources generated through some other business activity not subject to the same scrutiny and control their waste management business will entail. A company's major stockholders and Wall Street bond rating firms might have something to say about that, however, as will general market forces. Moreover, citizens and policymakers will insist on exacting regulation of private firms doing waste management work, and that invariably requires public agency involvement.

4. In allowing, or forcing, waste management organizations to go out of business, the nation would be resisting their institutionalization, thus contradicting Weinberg's assertion that institutionalization is both necessary and inevitable.

5. The quasi-experimental work of Elliott (1984) suggests that the concerns of the general public about the risks of hazardous facilities may not be entirely consistent with the political demand for error minimization. In communities proposed as sites for facilities, people appear more worried about detecting hazardous conditions that may arise and implementing mitigation measures speedily than they are concerned about preventing dangerous conditions from arising through sophisticated modeling and advanced technologies. The dominance of the politics of public risk by formally organized, self-proclaimed public interest groups that have helped to shape the regulatory process and then to use it effectively to forestall facility development as much as to ensure its safety may explain the discrepancy.

6. This is the conception of risk communications under development by Roger Kasperson and his colleagues in the Center for Technology, Environment, and Development at Clark University.

REFERENCES

Aberbach, Joel D. and Bert A. Rockman. 1978. Administrators' Beliefs About the Role of the Public: The Case of American Federal Executives. *Western Political Quarterly*, 31, 4:502–522.

Braitman, Jackie L. 1983. *Nuclear Waste Disposal: Can Governments Cope?* Santa Monica, CA: Rand Corporation (P–6942–RGI).

Burns, Jackie L. 1981. *Institutional Issues in the Planning and Implementation of a Program to Dispose of High-Level Radioactive Wastes*. Santa Monica, CA: Rand Corporation (N–1650–DOE).

Cook, Brian J., Jacque L. Emel, and Roger E. Kasperson. 1990. Organizing and Managing Radioactive Waste Disposal as an Experiment. *Journal of Policy Analysis and Management*, 8, 3:339–366.

Derthick, Martha. 1990. *Agency Under Stress: The Social Security Administration in American Government*. Washington, DC: Brookings Institution.

Easterling, Douglas. 1992. Fair Rules for Siting a High-Level Nuclear Waste Repository. *Journal of Policy Analysis and Management*, 11, 3:442–475.

Eisner, Marc Allen. 1991. *Antitrust and the Triumph of Economics: Institutions, Expertise, and Policy Change*. Chapel Hill: University of North Carolina Press.

Elliott, Michael L. Poirier. 1984. Improving Community Acceptance of Hazardous Waste Facilities Through Alternative Systems for Mitigating and Managing Risk. *Hazardous Waste*, 1:397–410.

Gruber, Judith E. 1987. *Controlling Bureaucracies: Dilemmas in Democratic Governance*. Berkeley: University of California Press.

Kaufman, Herbert. 1991. *Time, Chance, and Organizations: Natural Selection in a Perilous Environment*, 2d ed. Chatham, NJ: Chatham House.

Metlay, Daniel S. 1978. History and Interpretation of Radioactive Waste Management in the United States. In W. P. Bishop et al. *Essays on Issues Relevant to the Regulation of Radioactive Waste Management*. Washington, DC: U.S. Nuclear Regulatory Commission (NUREG–0412).

National Research Council, Commission on Geosciences, Environment, and Resources. 1990. *Rethinking High-Level Radioactive Waste Disposal: A Position Statement of the Board on Radioactive Waste Management*. Washington, DC: National Academy Press.

Paehlke, Robert and Douglas Torgerson. 1990. Toxic Waste and the Administrative State: NIMBY Syndrome or Participatory Management? In Robert Paehlke and Douglas Torgerson, eds. *Managing Leviathan: Environmental Politics and the Administrative State*. Kenmore, NY: Broadview Press.

Perrow, Charles. 1984. *Normal Accidents: Living with High-Risk Technologies*. New York: Basic Books.

Slovic, Paul, James H. Flynn, and Mark Layman. 1991. Perceived Risk, Trust, and the Politics of Nuclear Waste. *Science,* 254:1603–1607.

Smith, Randall F. 1980. *An Organizational Analysis of a Nuclear Waste Management System*. Seattle, WA: Battelle Human Affairs Research Centers (BHARC–311/80/010).

Sunstein, Cass R. 1990. *After the Rights Revolution: Reconceiving the Regulatory State*. Cambridge, MA: Harvard University Press.

U.S. Department of Energy. 1979. *Report to the President by the Interagency Review Group on Nuclear Waste Management*. Washington, DC (TID–29442).

———. 1984. *Managing Nuclear Waste—A Better Idea*. Washington, DC (DOE/NBM—5008164).

U.S. Office of Technology Assessment. 1985. *Managing Commercial High-Level Radioactive Waste*. Washington, DC: U.S. Government Printing Office (OTA–O–171).

Weinberg, Alvin. 1972. Social Institutions and Nuclear Energy. *Science*, 177, 4043:27–34.

Willrich, Mason and Richard K. Lester. 1977. *Radioactive Waste: Management and Regulation*. New York: The Free Press.

Wilson, James Q. 1989. *Bureaucracy: What Government Agencies Do and Why They Do It*. New York: Basic Books.

6

Managing Science: Quality Assurance and Nuclear Waste Disposal

AMY SNYDER MCCABE

In 1957, the U.S. National Academy of Sciences (NAS) determined that deep-mined geologic disposal of spent fuel and high-level radioactive waste (HLW) was technologically feasible, and a worldwide scientific consensus has since emerged endorsing the repository solution as optimal. Recent statements issued by international experts reaffirm support for the repository approach. At a 1989 meeting, Swedish scientists concluded that "[w]ith today's techniques the geological environment of the repository can be defined and its behavior predicted with much confidence" (Swedish Consultative Committee, 1991). The National Research Council Board on Radioactive Waste Management in 1990 emphasized that there is "no scientific or technical reason to think that a satisfactory geological repository cannot be built" (NRC, 1990). Most recently, a position paper issued by the Organization for Economic Cooperation and Development (OECD) and the International Atomic Energy Agency (IAEA) contends that current scientific methods are adequate to assess the safety and potential long-term radiological impacts of a waste disposal system on humans and the environment (OECD, 1991).

Many members of the science and engineering communities, while agreeing that geologic disposal is viable, qualify their opinions with an important caveat. They caution that it is impossible to predict, with a high degree of certainty, the behavior of a geologic formation over a period of thousands of years after facility closure. In their 1992 report to Congress and the secretary of energy, for example, Nuclear Waste Technical Review Board members emphasize that because of the extended time periods involved, technical uncertainties regarding the long-term performance of a repository wherever it is located will persist even under the best of circumstances (NWTRB, 1992). Engineers can design a system taking into account factors such as changes in groundwater chemistry; however, since specifics about future repository environments are unknowable, confidence in geologic disposal can be increased only by lowering levels of uncertainty (ibid.).

Performance assessments, which rely on complex computer models to describe how a system is likely to behave under a number of possible scenarios, will play a major role in reducing uncertainty associated with proposed sites. Data from laboratory and field experiments, coupled with information about natural analogues such as uranium deposits, provide the basis for model development and validation. In order for decisionmakers—particularly regulators—to evaluate future system performance, it is imperative that they have confidence in the detailed scientific information employed in these models. Appropriate quality assurance (QA) procedures, therefore, must be applied to data collection and carried out by project scientists.

QUALITY ASSURANCE, SCIENCE, AND HLW DISPOSAL

On July 8, 1991, the U.S. Department of Energy (DOE) broke ground at Yucca Mountain, Nevada, officially inaugurating the lengthy period of scientific investigation known as site characterization. DOE's objective at Yucca Mountain is to assess the integrity of geologic media to isolate radionuclides from the environment for a minimum of ten millennia, the length of time prescribed by regulatory requirements. Geophysical models of the site, based on data collected by DOE and its contract scientists, will be used to estimate facility safety during construction, operation, and closure. The results of this characterization effort, in addition to affecting DOE's ability to license the site, will set the future course for HLW management in the United States.

Because issues regarding QA will inevitably arise during licensing proceedings, quality assurance will play an integral role in the site characterization process. This invites the question whether DOE managers can effectively direct a QA program at Yucca Mountain, one that accommodates scientific uncertainty while meeting rigorous licensing requirements. It is the responsibility of DOE, under provisions of the Nuclear Waste Policy Act (NWPA), to comply with regulations promulgated by the Nuclear Regulatory Commission (NRC). To do so, DOE's Office of Civilian Radioactive Waste Management (OCRWM) must coordinate the activities of a large number of project participants, and ensure that contractors' work meets QA standards.

DOE's challenge is extraordinary on several counts. First, the organization has been assigned a task that is unprecedented in scope; that is, there are no prototypes in operation, and thus QA has not been tested in a repository licensing environment. Second, DOE is still adjusting to its new status as a regulated agency. Organizationally, it has had little experience with the implementation of complex regulatory schemes, such as the one prescribed for QA in the HLW program. Finally, program managers must develop and implement a QA plan that will satisfy the NRC, yet is perceived as legitimate by project scientists involved in the first-of-a-kind research endeavor. How the QA program is designed and implemented, then, will affect DOE's long-term organizational and operational effectiveness.

The latter problem—defining appropriate QA for research and development—has commanded recent attention because of a disagreement between OCRWM program managers and some project participants over how to apply QA at Yucca Mountain. The source of conflict is a philosophical and professional difference in how scientists and engineers approach QA in their working environments. This chapter explores the extent to which these divergent attitudes toward QA can affect the implementation of HLW policy. Its premise is that a QA program which is defendable in licensing proceedings will not come about unless managers understand the interpretation of QA by key scientific personnel and encourage the participation of scientists in the determination of QA standards. The following discussion seeks to elucidate the relationship between professional values and attitudes toward QA by examining how the socialization of scientists and engineers shapes their attitudes toward QA. An introduction to the meaning and purpose of quality assurance precedes a discussion of fundamental difficulties that public managers face when implementing QA in a research setting. Finally, the prospects for successful implementation of QA programs are offered.

QUALITY ASSURANCE IN THE ORGANIZATIONAL CONTEXT

The Evolution of QA in Organizations

How organizations define, measure, and achieve quality has been a topic of considerable interest from the onset of the Industrial Revolution. Contemporary quality assurance practices have roots in the principles of good workmanship and craftsmanship that characterized agrarian societies (Sinha and Willborn, 1985). With the explosive growth in manufacturing at the turn of the century came the recognition by the engineer Frederick Taylor that specialization of tasks led to increased productivity. Quality was measured in terms of meeting a performance standard, that is, quantity of output per time unit (ibid.).

The private sector, for many years, defined quality assurance as a mechanism to control cost through the inspection and rejection of manufactured goods. Quality control departments were held responsible for setting standards, and inspecting everything from raw materials to finished products. The underlying rationale for applying quality control to product design and development is that it is cheaper to "get things done right the first time." In this regard, QA is the guarantee that product manufacturers have subjected their work to strict quality controls, and that quality can be "achieved through prevention" (Fricke, 1991). While some argue that QA is not just quality control or inspection, these functions are widely perceived to be important features of an organization's quality assurance program (Hagan, 1968; Stebbing, 1989; Clements, 1990).

Just as predetermined standards help private companies monitor the quality and durability of manufactured goods, so have QA principles been applied to the public sector. The Department of Defense sponsored a study in the late 1950s that examined assurance of product performance and predicted probability of success for a given time period; the concurrent rise of the disciplines of maintainability and reliability engineering presumed that equipment would never be perfect, and downtime on account of repairs and maintenance would always be a necessity (Sinha and Willborn, 1985). Coming out of the defense experience, many nondefense government contracts require not only that organizations from which they procure products comply with the agency's QA regulations, but stipulate that suppliers have their own quality assurance programs as well (Sinha and Willborn, 1985; Fitzgerald and McCabe, 1991).

Still others trace the origins of quality assurance to the revolution in Japan's manufacturing sector following World War II. Based on techniques developed by the statistician Edward Deming and electrical engineer Joseph Juran, the Japanese adopted three key strategies to outperform their competitors: upper management would take charge of the effort and lead by example; employees at all levels in the organizational structure would be trained in quality management; and it was expected that quality would be improved on a continuing basis (Fricke, 1991).

The American hybrid—total quality management (TQM)—is a "strategic, integrated management system for achieving customer satisfaction. It involves all managers and employees and uses quantitative methods to improve continuously an organization's processes" (U.S. FQI, 1990). Total quality management is a philosophy as well as a set of guiding principles that has been adopted in various forms by many private and public sector organizations (Hyde, 1992). Participatory management and total employee involvement are fundamental requirements of a successful TQM program, and can only be achieved by breaking down barriers to quality, usually accompanied by a change in the organizational culture (U.S. FQI, 1990; Hyde, 1992). Quality assurance is a key aspect of TQM implementation, acting as a feedback mechanism for continual improvement over extended periods of time.

The Functions of QA

A review of this prolific literature quickly reveals the absence of a universal definition of QA. The interchanging of the terms quality assurance, quality control, and quality management contributes to a confusion about what exactly constitutes QA in principle and practice. At the same time, several trends relating to quality in organizations are readily identified.

First is the recognition by managers that QA can serve as a means to increase organizational accountability. Pressures from private sector stockholders, and in government, from the U.S. taxpayers, are incentives for managers to provide evidence that resources are producing desired results (Fricke, 1991). Quality assurance programs are thus useful as management tools to demonstrate compliance in program evaluations (Fitzgerald and McCabe, 1991). Second, it is apparent that the application of quality assurance programs is transcending product-based organizations. Although QA originated in the fields of manufacturing and engineering, there are increasing demands for service organizations and professionals to establish quantifiable standards of performance. This is particularly significant for certain professions—such as health care providers, lawyers, and research scientists—which traditionally have been semi-autonomous in defining quality assurance (Pollitt, 1990). Third, assuring quality in organizations requires a significant departure from the typical supervisor/worker relationship. The ability of management to orchestrate a change in organizational culture to accommodate employee involvement in setting quality goals lies at the very core of successful quality assurance practice. To create a climate which fosters employee empowerment, a minimum amount of faith that managers will actually relax control over the decisionmaking process is needed. Inherent in the process is a tacit understanding that management will actually take staff suggestions seriously. Developing this level of trust in a bureaucratic setting is especially challenging.

Finally, while QA programs are becoming more prevalent in organizations, the difficulty of crafting and putting into effect such programs is also rising. As with any program, effective implementation depends on the receptivity of the organization, the degree of complexity involved, and the willingness of decisionmakers to evaluate and make refinements. Quality assurance is thus an evolutionary process that must be continually appraised and improved upon. As such, there is a paucity of cases where the practice of QA has been empirically examined. This discussion turns to the application of QA to a highly controversial issue—the implementation of nuclear waste policy.

THE SIGNIFICANCE OF QUALITY ASSURANCE IN HLW MANAGEMENT

QA in the Nuclear Industry

In the engineering sciences, compliance with QA regulations is a common prerequisite to licensing by government entities. For the nuclear power industry, QA guidelines are issued by the Nuclear Regulatory Commission and serve a critical purpose in facility licensing. Documentation assures regulators that reactor plans were properly executed by allowing them to track site excavation and plant construction.

Failure to implement a stringent QA program can have consequences for nuclear utility managers ranging from relatively minor to severe. In January 1977 a Virginia utility was fined $31,900 for failing to follow NRC welding certification procedures and for other QA violations at the North Anna nuclear power plant site. Company officials testified at the operating license hearing that a management consulting firm had approved the utility's QA effort and that they had hired twenty-nine on-site QA personnel. During questioning by the NRC and the state's attorney, however, it was revealed that none of the consultants were available to testify, and that the additional QA staff were not put into place until both reactor units were virtually completed (Ames, 1978).

A more recent incident occurred in December 1990 when the decision was made to halt construction of a nearly completed unit at the Tennessee Valley Authority's (TVA) Watts Bar site because of persistent QA problems. The TVA, which suspended its beleaguered nuclear power operations in 1985, reacted by laying off about 5,800 employees; the agency then hired one engineering firm to take over the unit's construction, and another to deal with QA concerns. Nearly a year later the NRC approved TVA's request to resume work, but the project has been prolonged since a portion of the reactor must be rebuilt (*Nuclear News*, 1992).

The Need for QA in HLW Management

Quality assurance is critical to DOE's efforts to license an HLW repository at Yucca Mountain. In fact, of the myriad regulations included in the Nuclear Waste Policy Act (NWPA), few are as crucial to facility licensing as those mandating the implementation of a QA program. Section 121 (b) of NWPA directs the NRC to promulgate technical requirements and criteria that the agency will use to determine the approval of licenses for HLW repositories. Accordingly, Part 60 of Title 10 of the Code of Federal Regulations (CFR) establishes mandatory design specifications, as well as criteria for preclosure and postclosure performance to which DOE must adhere. Prior to sinking shafts at Yucca Mountain, for example, Subpart G of 10 CFR 60 requires that DOE develop a site characterization plan to the NRC. Under this directive, DOE must apply QA to all aspects of data collection and recording that deal with safety and waste isolation. Likewise, the agency is required to comply with applicable parts of "Quality Assurance Criteria for Nuclear Power Plants and Fuel Reprocessing Plants," found in Appendix B of 10 CFR 50 (Fitzgerald and McCabe, 1989). The DOE, in its 1988 Site Characterization Plan, states that quality assurance consists of "all the planned and systematic actions necessary to provide adequate confidence that a structure, system, or component is constructed to plans and specifications and will perform satisfactorily" (U.S. DOE, 1988).

Quality assurance in HLW management serves several additional purposes. First, QA is the central evaluative mechanism for demonstrating to state and local governments, regulators, and other stakeholders that the safety assessment is based on accurate scientific information (Fitzgerald and McCabe, 1991). The element of uncertainty associated with geologic disposal, which will remain for the lifetime of the project, calls for strict adherence to established QA procedures. Second, because of more open institutional arrangements, scientific and technical experts are being held to unprecedented standards of accountability, and becoming important actors in a frequently contentious political process. Thus, the demonstration by DOE of scientific integrity is especially relevant due to the state of Nevada's unwavering opposition to the characterization decision, and public consternation that continues to plague the program.

That DOE has traditionally been an unregulated agency is another concern that QA can address. From the inception of the nuclear waste program, the organization has suffered from perceptions that neither DOE nor its predecessor agency prioritized public safety, and that both were poor environmental stewards. The release of information in the last decade about environmental impacts of defense-related activities resulted in both a dramatic decline in public confidence in DOE and public demands that the agency be held to environmental standards at its nuclear facilities.

Yet a system failure with potentially catastrophic consequences is the most significant reason for subjecting repository construction to regulatory control. Most Americans eyewitnessed the *Challenger* tragedy in 1986, a grim reminder of what can occur when QA is mismanaged. An analysis of the *Challenger* accident revealed that "[t]he NASA/contractor system's autonomy obstructed discovery, monitoring, and investigation of safety hazards" (Vaughan, 1990). In this case, QA was compromised because of poor communication between contractors and NASA, as well as the internal regulatory structure that existed in the agency at the time (ibid.). Based on this experience, the odds of a catastrophe resulting from repository failure are likely to be greater under a self-regulating scheme. The possibility, however small, of the repository's failure to contain radionuclides is justification enough for regulating the DOE HLW program.

Considering this combination of factors, a flawless QA program will not assure success for DOE during the licensing phase, though a less-than-perfect QA effort could certainly disqualify Yucca Mountain as the agency's proposed site (Fitzgerald and McCabe, 1989, 1991). Even if the Nevada site is determined technically unsuitable, there are, however, clear political advantages to implementing quality assurance. A rigorous QA effort at Yucca Mountain, for example, could help build stakeholder confidence in the agency's ability to perform the HLW task at another site. DOE's QA program could be viewed as a unique opportunity to demonstrate organizational commitment to scientific rigor and regulatory oversight.

As discussed earlier, assuring quality in contemporary organizations requires a significant departure from traditional approaches to quality. In DOE's case, the consequences of not achieving an organizational commitment to quality are severe both in terms of program failure and total loss of stakeholder confidence in the agency's ability to implement HLW policy. Thus, the effectiveness of DOE's QA program depends in large part on the organization's willingness and ability to change the way it normally conducts business.

In essence, if QA is to serve as an asset to the agency, a "quality" culture will have to be forged within the organization. A commitment to quality must permeate the agency and spill over to the contractor organizations as well. The pivotal question, then, is whether DOE is capable of creating a climate that is conducive to an effective—that is, one that is acceptable to project participants and the NRC, and is legally defensible—QA program. To do so, the organization must have a clear understanding of QA goals, and develop a plan to accomplish those goals in conjunction with project participants. How well and to what effect DOE is able to do this will, in no small way, influence the site characterization process. The remainder of this discussion focuses on DOE's interaction with a very important group of project participants—the scientific community.

QA IN THE SCIENTIFIC CONTEXT: THE YUCCA MOUNTAIN EXPERIENCE

An Interdisciplinary Approach to the HLW Problem

Participants at a recent conference in Sweden were charged with the task of examining present scientific knowledge about HLW disposal and classifying information as either certain or uncertain, controversial or noncontroversial. In a report of the meeting, scientific experts stressed "that waste disposal strategy should be seen as an integration of methods and ideas which are interdependent and collectively focused on an inter-disciplinary approach to solve the many problems" (Swedish Consultative Committee, 1991).

The geologic and hydrologic testing to be conducted at Yucca Mountain requires the coordinated efforts of several disciplines. The magnitude of the scientific investigation is described by the General Accounting Office (GAO):

Site characterization includes extensive field and laboratory work to collect and evaluate geologic, hydrologic, geochemical, and other information. On-site work, for example, consists of surface-based activities, such as mapping, monitoring climate, and conducting geophysical surveys and seismologic and hydrologic studies. It also includes activities conducted in boreholes and trenches that will be used for ground water monitoring, core extraction, laboratory testing, and studies of the earth's geological structure and chemical composition and of underground water. Finally, studies will be conducted in the host rock through construction of an exploratory facility consisting of underground rooms and drifts (tunnels) excavated to and below repository depth through vertical and/or inclined shafts. (U.S. GAO, 1992)

Final engineering designs for the repository and waste package will be based on information gathered during site characterization. Hence, the process requires that earth scientists, performing basic research, work in conjunction with engineers from a variety of subfields.

The Problem with the Interdisciplinary Approach

This interdisciplinary approach to site characterization presents a challenge to DOE in that the agency must demonstrate QA compliance in a wide range of scientific and engineering activities. The problem for the agency is how to implement a QA plan that is perceived as legitimate by the scientific as well as engineering personnel, if the two groups view QA differently. The situation is exacerbated if agency management does not understand or fails to consider how professional socialization might compromise an interdisciplinary approach to QA.

The burgeoning literature on managing research and development suggests that scientists and engineers have different work goals and needs, and that managers should be aware of the differences. For example, one study that examined scientists' work attitudes found that scientists are "keenly interested in acquiring new knowledge, approach problems with a theoretical outlook," value the freedom to choose their type of work, report and publish results, and explore innovative methods of problem solving. Engineers were found to be more task oriented and their social values more similar to those of the organization's management than to those of the scientists (Badawy, 1971). Others warn that a failure to recognize "conflicting functional cultures" could be a barrier to achieving organizational goals, and that "risks are particularly high when changes require new behaviors and organizational structures, when decisions deal with complex technological choice, and when organizational inertia is a dominant factor" (Rosenthal, 1990).

Here lies the potential danger to the HLW QA program. Individuals naturally resent intrusion into their areas of expertise; scientific disciplines generally acknowledge the peer review process as a quality assurance safeguard, while most engineering projects conform with pre-established written standards. It is the responsibility of the administrator to gain a thorough understanding of each organizational function, and to create the structure within which problem solving takes place, identify the problems to be worked on, and review the recommended solutions (Hagan, 1968; Rosenthal, 1990). Evidence to date suggests the DOE QA program has not gone far enough in this regard.

QA: History and Status

How DOE managers can ensure the quality of scientific evidence gathered at Yucca Mountain is a topic that has received considerable attention for a couple of reasons. First, DOE determined in 1986 that much of the research conducted at Yucca Mountain since 1977 had proceeded in the absence of strict quality controls, and this caused the agency to impose a moratorium on further work until a proper quality assurance program was implemented. Then, complaints from sixteen hydrologists and hydrologic technicians about the application of QA to geological investigations were detailed in a 1988 memorandum to an assistant chief hydrologist at the U.S. Geologic Survey (USGS). The authors contended that:

It is also generally recognized that our current quality assurance (QA) program is modeled after the nuclear power industry's reactor facility QA guidelines. As a result, the present QA program is engineering oriented, inappropriate in most instances, and counterproductive to the needs of good scientific investigations. There is no facility for trial-and-error, for genuine research, for innovation, or for creativity. (Schneider, 1988:5)

Disagreements over the applicability of standard engineering QA procedures to site characterization led the National Research Council's Geotechnical Board and Board on Radioactive Waste Management to sponsor a QA colloquium in August 1988. In an introduction to the colloquium proceedings, two members of NRC's Geotechnical Board stressed the indispensability of QA for repository programs, that "the quality assurance program as it is being implemented is, in some ways, counterproductive," and that "if concerns of this type become general in the geotechnical and geological community it will adversely affect the ability of the repository program to continue to attract the scientific and engineering talents so necessary to the success of this unique program" (NRC, 1989).

This concern about far-reaching consequences for the Yucca Mountain site characterization has been echoed by program scientists. One individual observed that "ten years ago scientists were eager to join the site investigation team." Another former researcher warns that talented scientists are leaving the program because of overly strict QA requirements, and that there are "third and fourth quartile" scientists assigned to the project. In fact, six of the sixteen scientists who filed the complaint to the USGS have since left the program. The strict QA controls were seen as a disincentive to creative research, the basis of the scientific enterprise.

A series of meetings with the NRC and workshops with project scientists sought to alleviate the concerns over appropriate QA levels and approaches. The NRC accepted, with some exceptions, the QA programs of six DOE contractors in October 1990, and unconditionally approved these programs—as well as the DOE headquarters and Yucca Mountain Project Office programs—in January 1992. However, there are still several unresolved concerns.

First, there is a consensus among some members of the scientific and technical communities that the QA requirements remain prohibitively strict. Some feel that the DOE acquiesced to the NRC in the QA deliberations in its quest to push forward with site characterization. Nor has the issue over whether to accept peer review in the QA program been satisfactorily resolved. Some scientists are troubled that the peer review board, established to decide the appropriate QA needed, is composed of agency and contractor personnel who lack the necessary training to make informed judgments about geoscience issues. Finally, there is a perception that decisions about QA are still being made at a level too high in the organization, suggesting that DOE is unwilling to permit QA decisionmaking at lower levels. As one individual remarked, "It's not that QA hasn't been tested because no work is being done [at Yucca Mountain], it's that no work is being done because of the QA program" (personal interview, 10/16/92).

CONCLUSION: MANAGING SCIENCE IN A POLITICALLY CONSTRAINED ENVIRONMENT

In looking at quality assurance as a field of "urgent practical concern," Christopher Pollitt (1990) cites "a high proportion of prescriptive or exhortatory work resting on an apparently rather limited empirical base." This chapter sought to illuminate potential QA problems in an area of urgent practical concern—the implementation of HLW policy.

Underlying policy directives to construct repositories for spent fuel and high-level radioactive waste is the assumption that science can determine whether a geologic system can protect humans and the environment from radionuclide exposure for extremely long periods of time. Scientists' estimates about repository behavior are valid only if the data about the proposed site are of the highest quality. Assuring the quality of scientific and technical data used to assess the safety of a proposed site is a critical, yet often overlooked aspect of nuclear waste policy implementation that must be addressed no matter where a repository is located.

The definition of QA in private and public sector organizations is no longer limited to quality control. As such, the responsibility for QA cannot be delegated to a single department within an organization—it is the responsibility of management to ensure that products are designed and services delivered with quality as the primary goal. Thus, as Malcolm Baldridge asserts, "[f]or managers the challenge is to create an organizational environment that fosters creativity, productivity, and quality consciousness" (Roberts, 1983).

An examination of DOE's QA program offers a unique opportunity to observe the extent to which a public agency is capable of infusing quality principles into a large, complex hierarchical structure. The task is complicated because Yucca Mountain program participants represent a number of scientific and engineering subfields, and some of these professionals disagree on the definition and application of QA for research and development.

An effective QA process, therefore, depends on the ability of the DOE managers—both at the agency and program levels—to successfully forge a "quality culture" from existing disparate engineering and scientific cultures. The agency must simultaneously impose strict controls over all the processes that will determine the site's suitability, while providing procedural safeguards that do not unduly interfere with the creative process.

Whether DOE managers can develop the kind of relationship with their scientific personnel that fosters confidence in the QA process, at this stage of the process, is questionable at best. While there are signs of progress— many scientists admit that the DOE workshops helped researchers better understand the regulatory environment and industry views—others still regard DOE's QA requirements as overly restrictive for an experimental environment.

The probability that a QA culture will be created increases significantly if several areas are targeted. First, communication between the parties must be open and frequent. Because QA is an evolutionary process, QA workshops conducted on a regular basis should help resolve old concerns, as well as identify new ones. Second, standards for accepting peer review should be developed and implemented with the participation of the scientific community. Setting explicit peer review standards is a prerequisite for licensing, yet DOE has to understand that QA functions well only when employees truly participate in organizational decisionmaking and evaluation. Appointing more research scientists to managerial positions would be a positive step in that direction. Finally, evidence suggests that minimal intervention in, rather than total control over, QA functions reduces employee resistance to such programs (Pollitt, 1990). There is a spectrum of roles pertaining to QA that management can play, and DOE should reserve pre-emptory actions for areas where QA is most crucial.

Quality assurance, then, is a vital component of HLW policy implementation. How HLW managers react to the need for a total organizational approach to QA will significantly affect the chances for successful repository licensing, assuming the Yucca Mountain project proceeds. The application of quality assurance to a research endeavor, however, is just one of the scientific and technical challenges posed by HLW policy implementation. For example, are current risk assessment capabilities sufficient to meet Environmental Protection Agency and NRC regulatory standards? Does the current policy framework adequately provide for resolution of scientific disputes? To answer these questions requires not only management for innovation, but innovation in management as well.

REFERENCES

Ames, Mary E. 1978. *Outcome Uncertain: Science and the Political Process.* Washington, DC: Communications Press.

Badawy, M. K. 1971. Understanding the Role Orientations of Scientists and Engineers. *Personnel Journal*, 50:449–485.

Clements, Richard B. 1990. *Creating and Assuring Quality.* Milwaukee: ASQC Press.

Fitzgerald, Michael R. and Amy Snyder McCabe. 1989. Conflicts in Environmental Policy Administration: Quality Assurance in High-Level Radioactive Waste Management. Paper presented at the annual meeting of the Southern Political Science Association, Memphis, TN.

——. 1991. Conflicting Expertise and Uncertainty: Quality Assurance in High-Level Radioactive Waste Management. In John G. Heilman, ed. *Evaluation and Privatization: Cases in Waste Management.* San Francisco: Jossey-Bass.

Fricke, John G. 1991. Quality Assurance, Program Evaluation, and Auditing: Different Approaches to Effective Program Management. *Canadian Public Administration*, 4, 3:435–452.

Hagan, John T. 1968. *A Management Role for Quality Control.* Washington, DC: American Management Association.

Hyde, Albert C. 1992. The Proverbs of Total Quality Management: Recharting the Path to Quality Improvement in the Public Sector. *Public Productivity & Management Review*, XVI:25–37.

National Research Council, Commission on Geosciences, Environment, and Resources. 1990. *Rethinking High-Level Radioactive Waste Disposal: A Position Statement of the Board on Radioactive Waste Management.* Washington, DC: National Academy Press.

National Research Council, Geotechnical Board and Board on Radioactive Waste Management. 1989. *Quality Assurance Aspects of Geotechnical Practices for Underground Radioactive Waste Repositories: Proceedings of a Colloquium.* Washington, DC: National Academy Press.

Nuclear News. 1992. NRC Allows TVA to Resume Construction on Unit 1. January:25–26.

Nuclear Waste Technical Review Board. 1992. *Fifth Report to the U.S. Congress and the U.S. Secretary of Energy.* Washington, DC: U.S. Government Printing Office.

Organization for Economic Cooperation and Development. 1991. *Disposal of Radioactive Waste: Can Long-Term Safety Be Evaluated?* Paris: OECD.

Pollitt, Christopher. 1990. Doing Business in the Temple? Managers and Quality Assurance in the Public Services. *Public Administration*, 68 (Winter):435–452.

Roberts, George W. 1983. *Quality Assurance in Research and Development.* New York: Marcel Dekker.

Rosenthal, Stephen R. 1990. Bridging the Cultures of Engineers: Challenges in Organizing for Manufacturable Product Design. In John E. Ettlie and Henry W. Stoll, eds. *Managing the Design-Manufacturing Process.* New York: McGraw-Hill.

Schneider, Verne. 1988. Memorandum dated August 17 from sixteen hydrologists and hydrologic technicians, Nuclear Hydrology Program, Nevada Nuclear Waste Investigations to Verne Schneider, Assistant Chief Hydrologist for Program Coordination and Technical Support, U.S. Geologic Survey.

Sinha, Madhav N. and Walter O. Willborn. 1985. *The Management of Quality Assurance.* New York: John Wiley & Sons.

Stebbing, Lionel. 1989. *Quality Assurance: The Route to Efficiency and Competitiveness.* Chichester, England: Ellis Horwood Limited.

Swedish Consultative Committee for Nuclear Waste Management. 1991. *Is There A Definitive Answer? The Scientific Base for the Final Disposal of Spent Nuclear Fuel.* Swedish National Board for Spent Nuclear Fuel, Report 53.

U.S. Department of Energy, Office of Civilian Radioactive Waste Management. 1988. *Site Characterization Plan Overview.* DOE/RW–0198. Washington, DC: Department of Energy.

U.S. Federal Quality Institute. 1990. *Federal Total Quality Management Handbook: How to Get Started Implementing Total Quality Management—Part 1.* Washington, DC: Government Printing Office.

U.S. General Accounting Office. 1992. *Nuclear Waste: DOE's Repository Site Investigations, a Long and Difficult Task.* GAO/RCED–92–73. Washington, DC: General Accounting Office.

Vaughan, Diane. 1990. Autonomy, Interdependence, and Social Control: NASA and the Space Shuttle Challenger. *Administrative Science Quarterly*, 35:225–257.

Young, S. Mark. 1992. A Framework for Successful Adoption and Performance of Japanese Manufacturing Practices in the United States. *Academy of Management Review*, 17:677–700.

7

Transporting Nuclear Wastes: Securing Public Trust

LEONARD S. GOODMAN

Commercial fuel in this country is discharged from light-water reactors. The fuel from these reactors is made of uranium dioxide pellets typically contained within fourteen-foot tubes of stainless steel or zirconium alloy. A fuel assembly contains from 39 to 289 such rods. Spent fuel consists of these fuel assemblies following their use in a nuclear reactor. Since the fuel has become very radioactive, still producing some heat, spent fuel must be shipped in heavily shielded containers or "casks."

Spent fuel and other large quantity radioactive materials have been moving safely in interstate commerce for the past forty years. The safe transportation of large quantity radioactive materials did not occur by accident; it is a direct result of the careful design, construction, and regulation of the casks used in this transportation. Despite this impressive safety record, the perception of high-level risks associated with the transportation of radioactive materials persists, and there are signs that this, too, is not occurring by accident. This chapter considers some of the reasons for the misperception of risk—and what can be done about it.

SAFETY OCCURRED FIRST

The principles under which radioactive materials would be transported in interstate commerce were laid down long before any large quantity of radioactive materials were moved in this country. The effort began many years prior to such movements to solve practical problems relating to the distribution of radioactive isotopes for medical usage.

The creation of technical standards for shipping casks was set in motion by the Interstate Commerce Commission (ICC) as early as 1945. At that time the Oak Ridge National Laboratory (ORNL) announced it would begin shipping large numbers of radioactive isotopes by railroad express. The very conservative lead shielding then in use meant that many overly heavy and bulky shipments could result, which in turn created an immediate need for comprehensive review of the governing regulations. The National Research Council (the operating arm of the National Academy of Sciences (NAS)), headed by Dr. R. D. Evans of the Massachusetts Institute of Technology, completed a draft set of regulations for the Association of American Railroads (AAR). Based on the recommendations of the NAS and the AAR, the ICC published and later adopted regulations, which became effective in 1948.

Under these early regulations, certain principles were established that continue today. The rules (1) limited the maximum radiation level allowed to escape outside the package, (2) made certain that no radioactive material would itself escape the containment, and (3) provided that the containment must render the contents safe for transportation in regular freight service. The standards promoted safety by requiring a preshipment environment that ensured safe transportation in regular freight service without special handling requirements.

These early principles were subsequently adopted internationally. With the addition of hypothetical accident conditions now contained in the domestic and international regulations,[1] the underlying principles introduced by the NAS in the 1940s continue today as the essential approach to the safe transportation of radioactive materials.

SHIELDED CASKS

The containers that result from the international requirements (see Figure 7.1) are shielded casks that follow stringent design criteria and careful governmental evaluation before approval for use by truck or rail. There is no stronger container on the rails or highways of this country than the heavily shielded casks moving spent fuel and large quantity nuclear waste. With layer upon layer of stainless steel alternating with lead or depleted uranium, and impact limiters at either end of aluminum honeycomb or wood, they are engineered to withstand any credible accident scenario. Indeed, the studies performed at the Sandia National Laboratory of both scale models and full-scale casks placed the casks in severe accident environments without producing much more than superficial damage to them.

For example, Sandia conducted full-scale crash tests in the late 1970s with a locomotive moving at eighty miles per hour down a test track

Figure 7.1
Nuclear Waste Shipping Containers

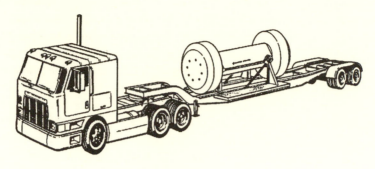

Truck Mounted Shipping Cask for Spent Fuel

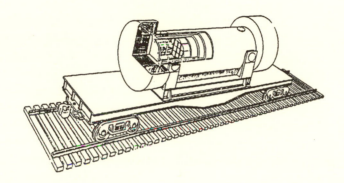

BR–100 Rail/Barge Shipping Cask

directly into a shipping cask mounted on a truck and trailer positioned across the tracks. The impact demolished the locomotive in the test and buckled the ends of its main beams; the cask suffered superficial damage without release of content (Huerta and Yoshimura, 1983). In another test a cask mounted on a railcar was crashed into a massive concrete barrier at eighty miles per hour. Sandia concluded that the typical spent fuel cask is "very rugged and able to withstand great impact forces" (ibid:33; and see Huerta, 1980).

When NRC asked the Lawrence Livermore National Laboratory to conduct a study to determine overall risk from transportation accidents, and to verify an earlier study (U.S. NRC, 1977), the laboratory produced the so-called "Modal Study" that concluded for broad classes of accidents, "spent fuel casks provide essentially complete protection against radiological hazards" (Fischer et al., 1987:xx).

UNBLEMISHED SAFETY RECORD

The end result of the collaborative efforts among the federal departments and agencies described above has been an unbroken, unparalleled safety record in the transportation of radioactive materials. In thirty-five years of shipping large quantities of radioactive materials such as spent fuel, there has never been a single injury or death attributable to any release of radioactivity. In 1986 the congressionally authorized Office of Technology Assessment (OTA) reported that the NRC performance standards produced a shipping cask "that provides an extremely high level of public protection, much greater than that afforded in any other current hazardous materials shipping activity" (OTA, 1986:109). It concluded "that the probability of an accident severe enough to cause extensive damage to public health and the environment caused by a radiological release from a properly constructed cask is extremely remote."

The OTA summarized some useful comparative accident data. The actuarial record, it reported, for the shipment of other energy commodities provides evidence of much greater risk and a consistent record of public fatalities. It reported an estimate of twenty-nine annual public fatalities associated with highway shipments of gasoline, fourteen associated with highway shipments of propane, and nine associated with rail shipments of propane. In contrast, the "record for public fatalities from spent fuel shipments to date is zero, and is estimated to be 0.0001 fatalities due to radiological factors per year with 2,000 shipments per year," that is, an infinitesimal rate that even then is "latent cancers calculated to occur over the life of the exposed individuals, as opposed to the prompt deaths associated with the other accidents" (ORNL, 1991:108–109).

Given this safety record, one would expect that the choice between modes of transportation for particular movements of spent fuel would involve only logistical and economic considerations. Unhappily, that has not always occurred.

RELEVANT LOGISTICS/ECONOMICS

Present truck casks can carry between one pressurized water reactor (PWR) assembly to seven of the smaller boiling water reactor (BWR) assemblies. Rail casks currently in service can carry between seven PWR assemblies and eighteen BWR assemblies, and weigh about seventy tons. The casks moving spent fuel for the Department of Energy/Department of Defense (DOE/DOD) are even larger. For future movements of cooler, commercial fuel to a permanent disposal site or to a monitored retrievable storage site, the truck casks may contain four PWR to nine BWR assemblies per cask, and rail casks may contain twenty-one PWR to fifty-two BWR assemblies per cask.

If a reactor site has both motor and rail capability, the economies of using rail transport, along with the reduction in overall number of shipments with the consequent reduction in total population exposure,[2] would seem to make rail transport the logical first choice for mode of transport. The railroad advantage is readily apparent from the available data. There were nearly 2,700 loaded casks of commercial spent fuel between 1964 and 1989 from the six sites for which data are available (namely, Hallem, Path Finder, Elk River, Fermi 1, Shippingport, and Peach Bottom 1). The rail shipments, which accounted for only 9 percent of the total number of shipments, nevertheless accounted for nearly one-half the spent fuel shipped (ORNL, 1991:8, 9). Adding to the railroad advantage, as we see from Table 7.1, was the fact that trucks were confined to hauling one cask at a time, whereas the railroads could, and often did, move more than one cask at a time.

Railroads have inherent cost and efficiency advantages in their ability to handle the larger loads. However, another factor today complicates those advantages, and threatens to convert a modal choice that should rest on logistical and economic considerations into a choice that merely avoids controversy. Perhaps the time has arrived, as I will next show, for shippers and carriers to apply a risk-benefit analysis to the avoidance of controversy.

LAGGING PERCEPTION OF RISK

While recognizing the extremely low risk associated with current transport of radioactive materials in shielded casks, OTA also recognized the public misperceives the risk. Notwithstanding the safety record, public attention focuses sharply on *any* accident, no matter how minor, involving

Table 7.1
Comparative Shipments, 1964–1989

	Motor	Rail
No. of assemblies	4,706.7	4,255.0
No. of shipments	2,346	230
No. of loaded casks	2,346	312
Weight (MTU)*	983.3	877.7

* One ton = 0.9072 metric tons

radioactive materials. OTA considers such a disparity common in the general public perceptions of risk.

I think there is more to it than that. The railroad industry has added to the misperception of risk; and while chiding the government for an alleged failure to educate the public to the high degree of safety involved in the transport of radioactive materials,[3] in recent years the industry has tended in its own actions to feed that misperception.

It was not always so. In 1962 the railroads operating in the South and West requested permission from the ICC to file tariff rates for the first time for the transportation of spent fuel. They pointed to the heavy metal shielding as providing "extremely adequate packaging." By the mid-1970s the railroad attitude took a sharp turn. Acting through AAR, their trade association, they now insisted that spent fuel and large quantity nuclear waste must henceforth move only in "special trains" at restricted speeds.

Although the railroads did not always agree on the operating conditions or the precise speed limit for the mandatory service that they envisioned,[4] they agreed that spent fuel should move in trains composed of cask cars, buffer cars, and a separate engine and crew segregated from all other rail freight traffic. The railroads never documented any rational basis for these mandatory special trains (lately called "dedicated trains") although given several opportunities to do so before the ICC. The new rail policy announced in the mid-1970s occasioned years of litigation by the electric utility industry and DOE/DOD with the railroad industry before the ICC and the courts, litigation that continues at the writing of this chapter.

The railroads generally concede that safety of shielded casks is not an issue. Instead a concern with public perceptions in part guides the rail industry's continued support of mandatory dedicated trains.

For example, during the 1987 Senate hearings on hazardous materials transportation, the railroad spokesman repeated over and over that special trains were needed simply "to satisfy public perception" or "in view of the uncertainty surrounding the transportation of nuclear material and the public perceptions of that transportation," or merely "to satisfy the concerns of the . . . public." When Senator John Danforth pointedly asked whether dedicated trains were "necessary for reasons beyond public relations," the rail spokesman suddenly maintained that a derailment with another commodity, if the radioactive materials moved in a mixed load freight train carrying "heavy equipment, flammable liquids, and many times, explosive commodities . . . could potentially have a devastating effect on a cask of nuclear material resulting in a release" (Dettmann, 1987:286, 287, 281). However, no evidence was produced to substantiate the claim that any credible transportation accident can breach a cask. Much less is it within the realm of realistic probability that any derailment, which in any event mostly occurs on slow speed, bad track, can result in a release.

The ICC, on the other hand, consistently held in several cases that mandatory special trains are wasteful transportation and an unreasonable railroad practice, providing no safety benefit.[5] This has not deterred the railroads from continuing to impose special trains on spent fuel shipments. In fact all commercial movements of spent fuel throughout the 1980s occurred in special trains; and it was not until 1989 that the government shipments of spent fuel for the Navy successfully avoided mandatory special trains, and paid no mandatory special train charges. The railroads have convinced Congress to require the Department of Transportation (DOT) to restudy the need, if any, for mandatory special trains and to report its findings to Congress under the 1990 Hazardous Materials Transportation Uniform Safety Act.

INFLUENCE OF SPECIAL TRAIN ISSUE

In 1985 the ICC warned the railroads that continued violations of its decision, which was that mandatory special trains were unreasonable, could result in enforcement penalties. While the ICC never sought any actual penalties, recently it ordered the railroads to refund millions of dollars of special train charges to the government for the period 1975 through 1988 with interest. It is not clear that the railroads are in any way chastened by this refund order.

There is compelling evidence in the meantime that the special train issue is having a direct effect on the public misperception of the transportation risk and even on transportation planning. I would go so far as to say that the railroads' continued insistence on special trains, despite their failure to convince the ICC of the need, is the single most compelling influence that promotes the current public misperception of transportation risk. Efforts to convince the public of the safety of the shipments are severely undermined if they are forced to move in that mode of service.

In a review of an article by Theodore Glickman and Dominic Golding (1992), Robert Jefferson and I describe the role that special trains played in literally scaring the public during the Three Mile Island (TMI) shipping campaign (Goodman and Jefferson, 1993). Once scared into believing special trains were needed, the public could not readily be "unscared" (compare Kasperson et al., 1988). The railroads' insistence on special trains aroused public concern and instilled the public misperception that for safety reasons the radioactive cars had to be isolated from all other traffic. Each minor mishap relating to the shipment thus became a *cause célèbre*.

The special train scare of TMI continued to affect the public perception of risk long after the completion of the TMI campaign. It has influenced Congress to require DOT to give more study to making special trains mandatory under the 1990 Hazardous Materials Transportation Uniform Safety Act; but that was in fact a compromise solution to a more severe remedy reported out by the Senate committee. The committee would have adopted the railroad position outright and imposed special trains on all spent fuel shipments in the reported version of S.2936. The committee's reasoning for this Draconian solution shows how a fear once sown breeds and grows.

The Senate committee did not adopt any of the reasons for special trains that had been asserted by the railroad spokesman at the hearings. Instead it thought that "mixed" trains would create complications for emergency response in the event of a serious accident—a fresh misperception that had not been heard before. Although special trains in fact were not needed for the purpose stated by the committee,[6] the public imagination had been inflamed by the introduction of the special train issue and the committee, embodying the public fear, invented a reason.

I mentioned earlier that a shipper of radioactive materials should expect that the expenditure to lease or develop the larger rail casks, rather than the smaller, lighter truck casks, would be offset somewhat by savings in shipping costs per assembly. The railroads have a distinct cost advantage over trucking companies in their ability to handle the larger casks. Mandatory special trains destroy that advantage. The special train charges are mileage charges. They have in the past increased shipping charges by rail for commercial shipments by many times. In a more recent statement presented by the DOE to the DOT Federal Railroad Administration, DOE showed that at the regular train rates requested by it before the ICC, the cost of mandatory special trains would enlarge total transportation costs ten times, and in one example seventeen times, over reasonable regular train charges.

RESTORING PUBLIC CONFIDENCE

This is a broad question, and I will attempt to make only three points. First, on a recent European trip, my wife and I were standing on the passenger platform of the rail station in a small Italian city, when a freight train pulling a group of tank cars of gasoline came through. I remember remarking, "Now, that's real risk"; I wondered how the public at large could be shown how much less relative risk was involved in radioactive materials transportation.[7]

In 1977, NRC computed the expected radiological consequences from the shipment of 3,000 metric tons of spent fuel per year at less than one latent cancer fatality every 2,300 years (U.S. NRC, 1977). Ten years later the Modal Study concluded that the risks were less than one-third the earlier estimate (Lahs, 1987:30; Goodman, 1988a). There is as yet no readily available manner of describing these extremely low risks in ordinary colloquial language in relation to other acceptable risks.

It would be useful to have an index of comparative risk in which acceptable risks would supply a benchmark and place the extremely low risks associated with transportation of radioactive materials in better perspective. We noted earlier OTA's summary of the relative numbers of annual fatalities associated with highway and rail transport of commodities like gasoline, propane, and chlorine, whereas there are none to date from spent fuel shipments, and only 0.0001 fatalities per year due to radiological factors (on the assumption that 2,000 casks move per year). Besides such low numbers, the index would have to grapple with the concept of "latent cancers" over the life of an individual as distinguished from the immediate deaths associated with other accidents. It is truly an unfinished task that deserves more attention. Such an index, I believe, would be a useful educational tool in the public discussion of these matters.

A second point is that in the early 1980s the railroads conceded before the ICC that there would not likely be any release of radiation in a railroad derailment, but for them that presented another problem. In the absence of a release, the Price-Anderson indemnification provisions would not apply, and the railroads would have to bear the potentially high costs of line closure while the accident was under investigation by conflicting governmental authorities. The railroads were unable to present any credible estimate of line closure time or its cost, so that the fear seemed to be based more on a lack of appreciation of the federal government's ability to respond quickly in a nuclear emergency. The ICC, therefore, dismissed this fear as exaggerated (U.S. ICC, 1986:657–658).

However, Congress responded with more sympathy for the railroads' argument in the 1988 amendments to Price-Anderson. It both extended the statute and expanded its coverage to include for the first time a "precautionary evacuation" initiated by an authorized state or local official to protect the public health and safety. The new phrase "precautionary evacuation" expressly includes "an evacuation of the public within a specified area near . . . the transportation route in the case of an accident involving transportation." Price-Anderson now protects persons liable for damage caused by such an evacuation, where such an emergency gives rise to a cause of action under state law.

We learn from this change in the law that the government will respond to the reasonable concerns of the railroads, when they define their concerns in a reasonably concrete manner.

Finally, when I talked to shipper personnel involved in commercial shipments of spent fuel during the mid-1980s, I was told they agreed to special trains to calm public fear. The railroads were insisting on special trains without any legal basis; but, supported by public fear and contract rates outside ICC jurisdiction, they convinced the shipper to agree to special trains. The traffic proceeded in special trains; yet the public would not be calmed. Like the TMI experience, it became impossible to explain to an aroused citizenry that the risks were minimal when the special precautions implied in the use of special trains dominated the news.

Public confidence has the best chance of recovery if shippers return to regular train service and choose rail service on purely logistical and other economic grounds. Mandatory special trains do not materially add to physical safety of the shipment, and more likely detract from it. In the meantime, they inflame and justify the public fear that these commodities must be segregated from all other freight.

DOE received thousands of requests for information regarding the TMI trains. I believe there would have been fewer inquiries, certainly not more, if regular train service had been used and the public had been shown that the casks could move with other freight without problems. Regular train service was never given a chance in the TMI campaign because one of the two participating railroads adamantly insisted on special trains.[8]

It is unclear that the public will always distinguish between the problems, let us say, relating to the massive clean-up of nuclear sites or the accident at TMI (or even Chernobyl) from the total lack of problems in transporting nuclear materials in regular freight trains. If it is perceived as one large problem, mandating special trains will not affect that perception. In the meantime, the negative effects of mandatory special trains will remain with us, and no positive effects can be expected.

The dispensers of at least governmental information should proceed on the assumption—because constructive response to the public's misperception is not possible on any other assumption—that the public misperception of transportation risk in time can be separated from its perception of all other nuclear risks. On that assumption, our best chance of regaining whatever public trust has been lost regarding transportation safety will be by insisting that radioactive materials should ordinarily move in regular freight trains, because the cask ensures safety in that mode of service and there is no need totally to segregate this traffic from all other freight. Having laid a proper foundation, we can then in a more consistent frame of reference renew efforts to educate the public on the strength of the container and the truly low risks of transport.

NOTES

1. The U.S. Department of Transportation and the Nuclear Regulatory Commission share the current responsibility for enforcement of the standards for transportation packaging. The DOT regulations are in Title 49 of the U.S. Code of Federal Regulations, Parts 173 and 174. The NRC regulations are in Title 10, Part 71. Under a memorandum of understanding between the DOT and the NRC (44 Fed. Reg. 38690, July 2, 1979), the NRC develops performance standards and reviews and approves package designs. DOT develops safety standards governing the carriers' handling and storage of the packages as well as standards for the lesser quantity (Type A) shipments.

2. The choice of routes by rail is relatively straightforward, since routes of rail movement must follow main lines and the better track, whether or not the shipments will flow through population centers. Efforts to route around cities risk more accidents, which, while posing no real safety threat, promise heightened media attention and the very real risk of inflaming public fear (for further discussion of this point, see Goodman, 1990:228).

3. For example, see U.S. GAO, 1987:57; and Dettmann, 1987:279, 281.

4. The Consolidated Rail Corporation, for example, insisted on running at a maximum speed of thirty-five miles per hour and stopping the special train when it met another train even if the other train was moving in the opposite direction on another track. The Union Pacific Railroad, on the other hand, chose a fifty-mile-per-hour speed limit and would stop the other train, letting the special train speed on to its destination. DOE and DOD argued before the ICC that no speed limit is necessary, except for nonsafety reasons on movements of defense shipments; and no stopping of trains was necessary, since a cask moves on ordinary flat cars without any clearance problems.

5. In a 1977 environmental impact statement by ICC and NRC staff, there was a finding that special trains in fact *increase* the nonradiological risk of injury and death simply by adding unnecessarily to total railroad train miles (ICC, 1977: Table 4.11 and Sec. 6). More recent work confirms that conclusion and indicates the nonradiological risk increases tenfold.

6. Under existing DOT regulations buffer cars already separate the radioactive cars from all other freight in regular, "mixed load," trains.

7. The same thought has occurred to others. The rail spokesman before Congress in 1987, for example, rhetorically wondered aloud that "in fact, most people apparently consider nuclear material to be much more hazardous than commodities that experience has shown to be more volatile, such as gasoline" (Dettmann, 1987:275).

8. In the end, GPU Nuclear, the owner and operator of the TMI site, decided to pay for the special trains to expedite the removal of the fuel in order to change the regulatory status of the inoperable reactor, and thereby save several million dollars.

REFERENCES

Dettmann, Charles E. 1987. Statement before the Subcommittee on Surface Transportation, Senate Committee on Commerce, Science, and Transportation. *Hazardous*

Materials Transportation. Hearings, May 12, 1987. S.Hrg. 100–147:271–281. Washington, DC: U.S. Government Printing Office.

Fischer, L. E., Chou, C. K., Gerhard, M. A., Kimura, C. Y., Martin, R. W., Mensing, R. W., Mount, M. E., and Witte, M. C. 1987. *Shipping Container Response to Severe Highway and Railway Accident Conditions*. Livermore, CA: Lawrence Livermore National Laboratory.

Glickman, Theodore and Golding, Dominic. 1992. For a Few Dollars More: Public Trust and the Case for Transporting Nuclear Waste in Dedicated Trains. *Policy Studies Review*, 10, 4:127–138.

Goodman, Leonard S. 1988a. Mandatory Special or Dedicated Trains for Radioactive Materials Shipments: Evidence Shows They're Not Needed. *Proceedings of the Symposium on Waste Management '88*. 2:399. Tucson: University of Arizona.

——. 1988b. *Source Book on the Safe Transport of Radioactive Materials in Regular Freight Trains*. Oak Ridge, TN: Science Applications International Corporation for the U.S. Department of Energy.

——. 1989. *Guide to Documents on the Safe Transport of Radioactive Materials in Regular Freight Trains*. Oak Ridge, TN: Science Applications International Corporation for the U.S. Department of Energy.

Goodman, L. S. and Garrison, Roy F. 1990. Routing Guidelines for Rail Transport of Radioactive Materials—Is Consensus Possible? *Proceedings of the Symposium on Waste Management '90*. 1:227. Tucson: University of Arizona.

Goodman, L. S. and Jefferson, Robert M. 1993. A Review of Resources for the Future's Reworking the Notion That Rail Transportation of Spent Fuel Must Occur in Dedicated Trains. *Policy Studies Review* (forthcoming).

Hazardous Materials Transportation Uniform Safety Act of 1990, P.L. 101–615.

Huerta, Michael. 1980. *Analysis, Scale Modeling, and Full-Scale Test of a Railcar and Spent-Nuclear Fuel Shipping Cask in a High Velocity Impact Against a Rigid Barrier*. SAND78–0458. Albuquerque, NM: Sandia National Laboratories.

Huerta, M., Dennis, A. W., and Yoshimura, R. H. 1978. *Impact Analysis of Spent Nuclear Fuel Shipping Casks*. SAND77–0466. Albuquerque, NM: Sandia National Laboratories.

Huerta, M. and Yoshimura, H. R. 1983. *A Study and Full-Scale Test of a High-Velocity Grade-Crossing Simulated Accident of a Locomotive and a Nuclear-Spent-Fuel Shipping Cask*. SAND79–2291. Albuquerque, NM: Sandia National Laboratories.

Kasperson, R. E., Emel, J., Goble, R., Hohenamser, C., Kasperson, J. X., and Renn, O. 1987. Radioactive Wastes and the Social Amplification of Risk. *Proceedings of the Symposium on Waste Management '87*. 2:85. Tucson: University of Arizona.

Kasperson, R. E., Renn, O., Slovic, P., Brown, H. S., Emel, J., Goble, R., Kasperson, J.X., and Ratick, S. 1988. The Social Amplification of Risk: A Conceptual Framework. *Risk Analysis*, 8:177.

Lahs, W. R. 1987. Transporting Spent Fuel, Protection Provided Against Severe Highway and Railroad Accidents. *NRC Summary of the LLNL Modal Study*. Washington, DC: U.S. Nuclear Regulatory Commission.

Lawrence Livermore National Laboratory. 1987. Transporting Spent Fuel, Protection Provided Against Severe Highway and Railroad Accidents. *NRC Summary of the LLNL Modal Study*. Washington, DC: U.S. Nuclear Regulatory Commission.

Oak Ridge National Laboratory. 1991. *Historical Overview of Domestic Spent Fuel Shipments—Update.* ORNL/Sub/88–997962/1. ORO/TOP–5405.0. Oak Ridge, TN: Science Applications International Corporation.

Price-Anderson Amendments Act of 1988. P.L.100–408. *U.S. Statutes at Large.* 102:1070.

Rack, H. J. and Yoshimura, H. R. 1980. *Postmortem Metallurgical Examination of a Fire-Exposed Spent Fuel Shipping Cask.* SAND79–1424. Albuquerque, NM: Sandia National Laboratories.

U.S. Congress. Office of Technology Assessment. 1986. *Transportation of Hazardous Materials.* OTA-SET-304. Washington, DC: U.S. Government Printing Office.

U.S. Department of Transportation. 1990. *Code of Federal Regulations.* Title 49, Parts 173 and 174. Washington, DC: U.S. Government Printing Office.

U.S. General Accounting Office. 1987. *Nuclear Waste: Shipping Damaged Fuel From Three Mile Island to Idaho.* GAO/RCED–87–123. Washington, DC: U.S. Government Printing Office.

U.S. Interstate Commerce Commission. 1947. Transportation of Explosives and Other Dangerous Articles, Docket No. 3666, Misc. Amendments. *Federal Register.* 12:7328.

———. 1962. (September 5). Twentieth Section Application of the Southern and Western Railroads to the Interstate Commerce Commission. (Unpublished).

———. 1977. (Staff) *Transportation of Radioactive Materials By Rail.* I.C.C. Final Environmental Impact Statement. Washington, DC: U.S. Interstate Commerce Commission.

———. 1978. Radioactive Materials, Special Train Service, Nationwide. *I.C.C. Reports.* 359: 70. Washington, DC: U.S. Government Printing Office.

———. 1980. Trainload Rates on Radioactive Materials, Eastern Railroads. *I.C.C. Reports.* 362:756. Washington, DC: U.S. Government Printing Office.

———. 1981a. Trainload Rates on Radioactive Materials, Eastern Railroads. *I.C.C. Reports.* 364:981. Washington, DC: U.S. Government Printing Office.

———. 1981b. U.S. Department of Energy v. Baltimore & O.R. Co. *I.C.C. Reports.* 364: 951. Washington, DC: U.S. Government Printing Office.

———. 1986. Commonwealth Edison v. Aberdeen & R.R., et al. *I.C.C. Reports, 2d Series.* 2: 642. Washington, DC: U.S. Government Printing Office.

U.S. Nuclear Regulatory Commission. 1977. *Final Environmental Statement on the Transportation of Radioactive Material By Air and Other Modes.* NUREG–0170. Washington, DC: U.S. Government Printing Office.

———. 1990. *Code of Federal Regulations.* Title 10, Part 71. Washington, DC: U.S. Government Printing Office.

U.S. Senate. 1990. Senate Report No. 101–449 on the Hazardous Materials Transportation Uniform Safety Act of 1990, 101st Congress, 2d Session, reprinted in *U.S. Code Congressional & Administrative News.* 7:4613–4615. St. Paul, MN: West Publishing Company.

Yoshimura, H. R. and Huerta, M. 1976. *Full-Scale Tests of Spent Nuclear-Fuel Shipping Systems.* SAND76–5707. Albuquerque, NM: Sandia National Laboratories.

8

Nuclear Waste Management in Sweden: Balancing Risk Perceptions and Developing Community Consensus

MARIANNE LÖWGREN

Risks attached to the management of nuclear power differ from those of fossil fuels and renewable energy sources in several ways. This was even more conspicuous two decades ago, when the problems of nuclear wastes entered the policymaking agenda. The Swedish environmental protection policy of the early 1970s focused on the abatement of local and well-defined substance emissions into air and surface water, mainly from large industrial and municipal point sources (Löwgren and Segrell, 1991). Management of nuclear wastes posed a new set of threats and questions. Society faced intangible damages of radiation in a diffuse time and space perspective. The time perspective was (and is) inconceivable to man—how can safe deposits be created that will last for hundreds of thousands of years? Genuine uncertainty exists about safety. How safe is safe enough, and which experts can be trusted?

In this paper the political process is viewed as the interface, where the credibility and the legitimacy of scientific and economic experts' judgments are questioned and confronted with oftentimes obscure underlying social dimensions of environmental risk. In the late 1960s the five political parties that were established in the Swedish Parliament generally responded slowly to growing public concerns about environmental issues. Many people mobilized in nongovernmental organizations; some engaged locally in rather informal protest groups against exploitations of nature, others joined existing conservation organizations or new environmental protection movements, but gradually environmentalism extended into the Parliament. For reasons that will be discussed below, energy policy and its ramifications became key issues, and nuclear waste management in particular became a stumbling block in Swedish politics in the late 1970s.

NATIONAL NUCLEAR POLITICS

Nonmilitary development of nuclear power in Sweden was initially stated in the 1956 Atomic Law, and for almost two decades it was approved by all political parties. During the 1950s and 1960s energy consumption increased 4 to 5 percent annually. After this unprecedented period of economic growth, Sweden achieved an enormous increase in living standards, and there was no doubt that the increased use of energy, mainly oil, had been a crucial factor.

Sweden's first commercial nuclear reactor was ordered in 1966, and between 1970 and 1971 the Swedish Parliament (Riksdagen) unanimously adopted plans for eleven reactors to be operating by 1980. The need to find new sources of energy seemed obvious enough, and the nuclear energy program appeared to offer cheap, ample, and clean energy supplies. Low energy cost was demanded by important Swedish export industries, for example, paper and pulp plants, and iron and steel works. The commercial potential of the new technology challenged engineering companies, and close cooperation between government and business evolved. Sweden's uranium deposits at Ranstad were significant in size, and from the government's point of view national control over the whole cycle of energy production was highly desirable. The blocking of trade during World War II had clearly demonstrated the vulnerability of a small nation's economy. Even conservationists agreed to the nuclear power program because it meant that energy supplies could be expanded without the exploitation of the few remaining pristine rivers in the northern part of the country (Lewin, 1988).

The economic situation changed dramatically in 1973. The oil crisis of 1973–1974 caused an international recession, and the golden years of Sweden's economic growth ended. With the recession came a political backlash. The economic policies of the ruling government (Social Democrats) had vigorously sponsored the restructuring of industry based on cheap energy costs and by facilitating the mobility of labor during the 1960s. Finally, however, urbanization, large-scale production, and high technology lost some of their allure for the people. In Parliament the backlash movement was first captured by the Center Party (former Agrarians), which adopted an ideology of small-scale production, environmental protection, and regional balance. This "green wave" moved the Center Party into the role of the leading opposition party, collecting 25 percent of the votes in the 1973 election. Nuclear power generation became the symbol of a centralized, elitist, and high-tech development of society, the opposite of the new visions of the Center Party. Indeed, a Center Party member of Parliament triggered an intense public debate on the ethical aspects of nuclear waste disposal. In Fall 1972 she questioned the "moral defensibility" of a nuclear program which would place heavy burdens on future generations.

The Center Party succeeded in forcing a moratorium on further reactor licenses in 1975 and the still-ruling Social Democrat government had to prepare a comprehensive energy policy statement. The energy proposal continued the Social Democrats' commitment to a high-energy, high-technology policy. They proposed the construction of thirteen reactors (which set the stage for political controversy). In addition, the government proposed the transfer of reactor licensing decisions from licensing authorities to the Parliament. Both actions indicated the political significance of the nuclear strategy in Sweden's national politics.

In the election campaign of 1976, the leader of the Center Party vigorously and successfully fought against nuclear power. In 1976, the Social Democrats were defeated after forty-four years of government. Certainly there were other crucial issues in the defeat of the Social Democrats, most notably a strong nonsocialist resistance against the introduction of wage-earners funds proposed to be controlled by trade unions. However, to a large extent this historic overturning of the Social Democrat Party rule in the 1976 election was due to the appeal of the Center Party's strongly antinuclear platform. Following the 1976 results, the Center Party, the Liberals, and the Conservatives formed a nonsocialist government coalition. Considering their diverging opinions about the future development of nuclear power, troubled cooperation could be expected: the Center Party proposed five reactors operating in 1985, the Liberals wanted eleven, and the Conservative Party, thirteen to fourteen. Swedish nuclear policy would now be shaped by a series of compromises.

The first compromise focused on waste disposal safety: the new government declared that reactors under construction were not to be fueled until an "acceptable" contract for the (foreign) reprocessing of spent fuel and an "absolutely safe" technique for terminal storage were demonstrated. A new piece of legislation, called the Stipulation Act, made the holders of licenses for nuclear reactors formally responsible for totally safe handling and final disposal of all radioactive wastes. This act quickly limited the range of options for ultimate disposal of high-level wastes (HLW). Disposal at sea or to space and transmutations (e.g., glassification or reprocessing) no longer were feasible methods.

Very soon after the Stipulation Act was published in December 1976, the utilities launched a major research program into HLW disposal: the Nuclear Fuel Safety Project (KBS).[1] Over 400 researchers worked for

eighteen months to cover all vital aspects of the nuclear fuel back-end cycle
with an emphasis on long-term geological, hydrological, and geochemical
effects. The final report, based on fifty-eight volumes of national and
international experts' investigations, proposed a method for satisfying the
conditions set by the Stipulation Act. Briefly, the following procedure was
suggested: after a thirty-year period of cooling, spent nuclear fuel was to
be deposited in rock about 500 meters underground in sealed metal
canisters. The canisters would be surrounded by a number of technical and
natural barriers to prevent radioactive substances from reaching the
groundwater for 200,000 years.

The outcomes of the KBS project were scrutinized by a wide spectrum
of experts and laymen, and several conflicts about proofs and safety
evolved. The KBS report was criticized for presenting overly cautious
performance assessments of the method chosen, introducing the concept
of "acceptable risk." The emphasis was laid on engineered barriers rather
than natural geological barriers. Frans Berkhout (1991) ascribed this
strategy to two political functions of the plan. Man-made barriers can be
manipulated, tested, and controlled to an extent not possible for natural
conditions. Besides, hydrogeological and geochemical information necessary for a safety analysis was not yet available. Second, the multibarrier
repository concept was introduced, and theoretical redundancy was incorporated to enhance resistance against waste dissolution and radionuclide
transport. Overdesign had its persuasive function in increasing the plausi-
bility and trust in the process of gaining public acceptance for nuclear
waste repositories.

Despite the massive scientific effort to fulfill the necessary conditions
for the continuation of the nuclear program, a political dilemma remained.
A major conflict arose among the Center Party on one side and the Liberals
and the Conservatives on the other concerning the interpretation of the
Stipulation Act, a conflict that paralyzed decisionmaking about the fueling
of two new reactors which were finished in 1978. The Center ministers
opposed the fueling for three reasons. First, they refused to accept the
reprocessing contract, because the French reprocessing plant was not yet
built. Second, they claimed that the applicant company did not succeed in
showing a spot where the ground was solid enough to allow a safe final
deposition of wastes. Third, the plutonium that would result after the
reprocessing was not accounted for.

After long discussions the Liberals and the Conservatives reluctantly
accepted the second point. However, they held the opinion that the other
objections were beyond the scope of the Stipulation Act. The Liberals and
Conservatives could agree on a temporal refusal for the fueling permits in

order to save the cabinet, but they did not want to stop the future development of the nuclear program, which was the key issue of Center politics. This profound disagreement about energy policy caused the resignation of the prime minister, Torbjörn Fälldin, in October 1978, and brought the termination of the first non–Social Democrat government since the 1930s (Vedung, 1979).

A new minority Liberal government came to power and the next general election produced a new nonsocialist government, once again led by Center leader Torbjörn Fälldin. After the accident at Pennsylvania's Three Mile Island (TMI) nuclear plant (March 1979), the Social Democrats, Liberals, and Conservatives shifted their preferences in a direction more critical to nuclear power, and they agreed to the referendum which the antinuclear movement had demanded since 1973. In a nationwide referendum, held on March 23, 1980, Swedish voters chose among three options concerning future development of nuclear power:

- Alternative 1 (supported mainly by the Conservatives): Yes, nuclear reactors must be used to reduce our dependency on oil imports in order to maintain employment and economic growth. Until renewable energy sources become available, twelve reactors (the ones presently operating or under construction) should be used, but the last one should be shut down no later than 2020.

- Alternative 2 (supported by the Social Democrats and the Liberals): Yes, similar to Alternative 1 regarding the scope of the nuclear program, but also a strong emphasis on energy conservation, environmental safety measures, and accelerated research on the development of renewable energy sources and a phase-out no later than 2010.

- Alternative 3 (supported by the Center and the Left Communist Party): No, the use of the present six reactors should be phased out within ten years with no more construction. Instead, investment in renewable energy sources and energy conservation would be substantially increased.

Three-quarters of the electorate cast their votes. Alternative 1 was preferred by 18.7 percent of the voters, Alternative 2 received 39.4 percent of the votes, and Alternative 3 received 38.6 percent. Another 3.3 percent indicated their dissatisfaction with the options by casting a blank vote. This resulted in a decision to end nuclear power generation no later than the year 2010. The number of reactors should not exceed twelve, and, since

1985, all are operating in plants located along the coasts of southern Sweden (Figure 8.1). Two plants are situated on the West coast (Ringhals and Barsebäck), and two are on the East coast (Oskarshamn and Forsmark).

OPINIONS ABOUT NUCLEAR WASTES

According to Brian Wynne (1987), people respond to nuclear technology, including risky artifacts like radioactive wastes, nuclear reactor accidents, and nuclear weapons, in a highly emotional dimension. Such issues are perceived as dreadful, highly risky to future generations, involuntary, and uncontrollable. On a cognitive dimension the unfamiliarity—that is, the low degree of observability, the lacking of knowledge of those exposed, and risks unknown to science—scores high for radioactive wastes and nuclear reactor accidents. Quite consistently, nuclear war was classified as more familiar, although more dangerous. Further, Wynne places individual psychological reactions into a societal context: risk perceptions not only reflect individual and subjective mental states, they also incorporate social experience from earlier technical innovations where the public has questioned institutions designed to manage a new technology. There may also be serious concerns about lack of control over present and future decisions, and over distributional effects based on differing social realities of trust and power. Thus, a far more complex picture of nuclear waste disposal problems appears, differing from views held by proponents of "rational" and "objective" risk management exclusively based on statistical probabilities.

The 1970s saw Sweden's first battle over nuclear policy. During this period the opponents mainly raised various problems of waste disposal. Waste management was the dominating negative argument both in the media and among the public. After the TMI accident, and in the campaigns preceding the referendum, other threats, most notably reactor accidents and meltdowns, attracted more attention. Yet Sören Holmberg (1990) shows that through the 1980s the waste disposal issue was still the predominant argument against the nuclear program. In a 1986 survey a large proportion of the Swedish population expressed their doubts about the possibility of depositing nuclear wastes safely: 45 percent did not believe that nuclear wastes could be treated and stored in a safe way for the next fifty years, and 52 percent responded negatively when a longer time perspective was considered. In contrast, when surveying members of the Parliament in 1988, Holmberg found that only 17 percent did not believe that short-run waste disposal could be handled safely, and only 28

Figure 8.1
Swedish Nuclear Power Stations

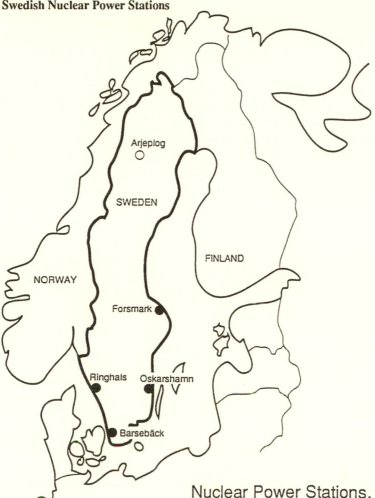

Nuclear Power Stations, 1990

Site	Capacity, MW	Start
Oskarshamn 1	440	1972
Oskarshamn 2	600	1974
Oskarshamn 3	1150	1985
Ringhals 1	820	1976
Ringhals 2	860	1975
Ringhals 3	915	1981
Ringhals 4	915	1983
Barsebäck 1	600	1975
Barsebäck 2	600	1977
Forsmark 1	970	1980
Forsmark 2	970	1981
Forsmark 3	1150	1985

percent responded negatively concerning the long-term safety of HLW disposal. These figures indicate that the general public was clearly more worried about nuclear waste management safety than were government decisionmakers.

As was mentioned before, the Stipulation Act requires the producers of radioactive wastes to provide safe deposition facilities. For the disposal of HLW the KBS project outlined a repository to be located in unfractured granitic bedrock 500 meters below the surface. The search for suitable areas started in 1978, when studies of geological properties were initiated in five different locales. As could be expected, test activities met with local opposition and generated classic not-in-my-backyard (NIMBY) protests (Kraft and Clary, 1991) as residents learned of the purpose of the investigations. The most enduring NIMBY protest has taken place in Kynnefjäll, a mountain area on the West coast, not far from the Norwegian border. A local group was formed in 1979 with the objective of resisting every attempt to perform test drillings for final deposition facilities at Kynnefjäll. Indeed, since April 23, 1980, local inhabitants have guarded the road leading into the mountain area at Kynnefjäll (Lidskog and Elander, 1990).

After the Chernobyl accident, in the second battle over nuclear power, waste management played a less important role in the public debate. Parts of the northern and eastern Swedish territory received a considerable amount of radioactive deposits from the Soviet accident, which did of course evoke great immediate anxiety about health effects. Economic losses appeared; for example, the sales of milk and products from the rearing of reindeer in the far north were prohibited for a period. Recreational amenities were reduced because of recommended limitations for the consumption of hunting game, fish, mushrooms, and garden products. After some time, however, risk awareness declined. No effects were to be seen, and in the late 1980s, public attitudes again turned in a direction somewhat more favorable to the use of nuclear power in Sweden.

The Swedish case indicates a correlation between attitudes toward nuclear power in general and judgments about risks related to its waste management. According to Holmberg (1990), the final deposition of nuclear wastes is perceived as a dominant risk, showing the same magnitude as the risk for a spread of nuclear weapons. Indeed, these two risks are judged to be definitely higher than risks for genetic damages, environmental damages, increasing numbers of cancers, or a reactor accident in Sweden. In addition, while estimations of these latter risks have all fallen during the 1980s, risks connected to the final deposition of wastes have decreased by only half as much. To explain this fact, Holmberg suggests that final waste deposition risks were not actualized by the Chernobyl accident to the same extent as other risks (environmental damages, cancer incidences, reactor accidents). As the Chernobyl effect faded away, the judgments of final deposition risks thus were less affected than the other risks mentioned.

Attitudes toward nuclear wastes also differ among regions, ages, and sexes. Women, young persons, and people living in the northern part of the country and in the two biggest cities ascribe a higher risk to final deposition than do men, older persons, and the population of southern Sweden. There also is a correlation with political party affiliation, though not entirely along the traditional "red–blue" or leftwing–rightwing dimension. Rather, a new "red–green" coalition thrived in the 1970s and early 1980s on a dimension ranging from an adherence to economic growth as opposed to subordination under ecological restrictions. The Social Democrats clustered around the growth ideology together with Conservatives and Liberals, while the Centers, the Left Communists, and the coming Green Party united around what they viewed as ecologic imperatives (Vedung, 1979). Consequently, people sympathetic to the Left, Center, and Green Parties are more concerned about the risks of nuclear waste disposal than Social Democrats, Liberals, and Conservatives. The difference, however, is smaller than the difference of opinions about the nuclear power program generally. This might be interpreted to indicate that final deposition risks have not yet been affected by strategic political considerations within the parties to the same extent as the nuclear power program. Further, Holmberg (1988) relates the degree of knowledge about the nuclear program and the nuclear policies of the political parties to risk judgments. The correlation is very regular, indicating that a lack of knowledge is accompanied by a high level of risk awareness. Due to the rather shallow way of measuring knowledge in this study, however, such a correlation should not be the base for simplistic conclusions about nuclear waste management risk perceptions as being primarily a matter of lacking information.

IMPLEMENTATION OF WASTE DISPOSAL FACILITIES

A site search program started in 1978 for a central spent-fuel store. By constructing a central spent-fuel store, the utilities paved the way for a new direct disposal concept. The KBS–2 program proposed a sea-transport system, a copper-canister design, and spent-fuel disposal starting in 2020, all of which later became adopted as policy. No explicit decision was ever made, but from 1979 the idea of reprocessing gradually disappeared due to lack of support from government and the industry. The move to a "throw-away" fuel cycle had the decisive effect of simplifying the implementation of the back-end strategy and clarifying the objectives of waste management. A new organization was set up in 1980 to administer a fee levied on nuclear electricity to finance waste management, decommissioning, and disposal. KBS–3, the final fuel-safety report, was submitted in May 1983. The strategy closely followed that of KBS–2, namely, centralized storage of spent fuel for forty years, encapsulation of spent fuel in copper canisters, and deposition of wastes in two separate repositories. A little later the central condition of the Stipulation Act was revised. Now the reactor owners have to demonstrate that a method exists for the handling and final disposal of nuclear wastes that can be approved with respect to safety and radiation protection. That revision confirms the notion of the KBS programs as principal solutions rather than projects with simply site-specific applications.

The 1980 referendum propelled the development of an energy program addressing key issues of nuclear power, the outline of which in terms of size and time duration became defined and settled at an early stage. As a result the Swedish nuclear industry has made better progress than that of most other countries in establishing waste disposal facilities. Two repositories have been sited. One is the Central Final Repository (SFR) for low-level wastes (LLW) and intermediate-level wastes (ILW), operating since 1988. The other one is the Central Interim Storage Facility for spent nuclear fuel (CLAB), which started its operation in 1990. There is reason to believe that the Swedish nuclear industry has learned some lessons from these projects that will be useful in the process of identifying a suitable site for the final storage of HLW. The SFR is located in Forsmark, one of the nuclear power plant sites, because this time the Swedish Nuclear Fuel and Waste Management Company deliberately confined its search for a suitable location to one of the existing four nuclear power sites where they have good relations with local authorities. The nuclear power plants are important employers and they do a profitable business, which is equally appreciated by local governments and the workforce. The employees are well educated and trained to deal with radiation protection, so the resistance to nuclear energy is less pronounced than elsewhere. Waste transports are simplified as all the reactors are coastally situated and could be linked by boat. Forsmark was also chosen because the new construction project was a suitable successor to the third reactor construction that was just completed (Kemp, 1991). CLAB, the first interim storage facility for HLW, is located in Oskarshamn, for similar reasons. Capacity for the storage of spent fuel is guaranteed at CLAB until at least 1994. According to the plans, a series of studies will be carried out to make detailed characterizations of two possible sites, the final decision of which will be made around the turn of the century. The construction period must not start until 2010, so there is time to prepare the ultimate siting decision.

NUCLEAR WASTES IN THE 1990s

Will there be a third battle over nuclear power? For a fact, wastes which have been generated for years must be taken care of, and the decision about the localization of final deposition of spent nuclear fuel is still pending. Combined with a number of significant circumstances this may lead to a political comeback of the nuclear policy issue—or a suppression of potential conflicts. Some smoothing mechanisms are embedded in the regulatory set-up. Swedish nuclear waste management policy is characterized by a simple and independent regulatory framework aimed at promoting consensual decisionmaking with mechanisms that might limit political contentiousness. The Swedish Nuclear Fuel and Waste Management Company (SKB) was founded in 1980 by the four Swedish nuclear industries. SKB has the task of implementing the waste management strategy under the supervision of three government authorities: an independent administrative agency called SKN (the Swedish National Board for Spent Nuclear Fuel); SKI (the Swedish Nuclear Power Inspectorate), which is responsible for the coordination between nuclear facilities and repositories; and SSI (the Swedish Institute for Radiation Protection). SKI, SSI, and SKN each have a board of political nominees who represent various sectors of society. The principle of a wide representation of different interests is a fundamental feature of Swedish political culture, aiming at the creation of comprehensiveness and public legitimacy in decisionmaking. Politically appointed boards to independent governmental agencies are one of the prime means by which the inclusive and consensual style of policymaking is transferred to the administrative sphere, while the interference of sponsoring ministries is strongly resisted.

Sweden's nuclear waste policy was founded in the middle of strongly conflicting political objectives. However, several features of the political context have changed since the early days of public protests against the consequences of the nuclear program. During the 1980s the Swedish Parliament saw some dramatic transformations. The long-established party structure changed as two new parties formed and took seat. The Green Party entered in the 1988 elections by managing to attract more than 4 percent of the votes (which is the limit for parliamentary representation). This was a remarkable event in Swedish political life. However, the peak of environmentalism passed rapidly. Three years later the Greens were not reelected, and, more importantly, after the 1991 elections the Social Democrat government was again replaced, this time by a coalition of Conservatives, Liberals, Centers, and a new party, the Christian Democrats. The Conservatives always were the leading proponents for a Swedish nuclear power program, and the party now represents almost one-quarter of the electorate. The current political platform for the new prime minister, Carl Bildt, a Conservative, is European economic integration. Most political parties agree that Swedish membership in the European Community is necessary from an economic point of view. Currently, (Summer 1993) Sweden is still suffering from the effects of the recession of 1990–1992, and national fiscal efforts are being made to stimulate economic growth and competitiveness in international markets. Under these circumstances it is likely that energy policy priorities will be reviewed as the year 2010 approaches. Still, the task might be delicate for the present non–Social Democrat government coalition as the Centers and the Liberals tied themselves closely to the abolition of nuclear power generation after the referendum. But the economic argument is strong now: 45 percent of the Swedish electricity production came from nuclear stations in 1990, compared to 3 percent in 1976. Industry could well argue that it would be foolish to close down facilities that could economically and technically serve their purpose for a longer period of time in a country with high technological capabilities and strict safety regulation, at least compared to those in some of its new neighboring countries.

Many official evaluations and research programs on various aspects of energy policy were performed during the 1970s and 1980s. For example, from 1973 to 1980, approximately forty official government commissions (*utredningar*) worked on different aspects of energy policy, and in 1980, research within the energy sector took 10 percent of total Swedish research and development costs (Wittrock and Lindström, 1984). The development of renewable sources of energy attracted a vivid interest from many researchers, environmentalists, and media outlets. Still, by the end of the 1980s no economically feasible substitutes exist to replace the main part of the dependency on nuclear power. This may partly be ascribed to a half-hearted political backing of new alternatives. Seemingly rational administrative behavior, including scientific research and official committee work, is a traditional Swedish way of easing political deadlocks and postponing controversial decisions at least for some time. In 1977, through the Stipulation Act, the responsibility of nuclear waste management was transferred from the state to the nuclear industry, and ever since, important choices in nuclear waste strategy have been made by the utilities themselves, often at some distance from the political establishment. In the 1979 elections the Conservative Party replaced the Center Party in the position as the largest nonsocialist party, and, as was noted before, their pronuclear attitudes were shared by the Social Democrats, who won the 1982 elections. Although little heard of during the intense environmental debate of the 1980s, such undercurrents are important for the creation of informal networks, aimed at coordinating political and industrial interests.

In developing policy concerning the risks inherent to nuclear waste management, two aspects are vital. One is the general reevaluation of environmental problems that has occurred since the 1970s. Two decades ago nuclear wastes were outstanding in their mysterious large-scale and long-term potentially harmful environmental effects, while "normal" environmental problems were local, caused by point-source emissions of mostly well-known substances from municipalities and industries into air and water. However, during the 1980s environmentalist conceptualizations widened. The consequences of several intended and unintended material flows were recognized to have negative environmental impacts, some of which were regional or even global (Löwgren and Segrell, 1991). Acidification, ozone depletion, and greenhouse effects all became part of common knowledge. This process has shed a new light on the pros and cons of various alternatives for energy production, and for the moment energy conservation just is not a politically viable option.

The other aspect is the increasing familiarity in society with risks (and benefits) attached to various uses of nuclear matter, not only in the power industry but also for medical treatment and research programs. More attention is now being paid to other sources of radiation. As the acquaintance with nuclear processes and their side effects has increased, the implication is that the position of nuclear wastes "within the radiation family" is slowly changing. Proponents of nuclear power have long claimed that man has always been exposed to radioactive radiation from natural sources, and that the extra contribution from nuclear energy systems and other manmade sources is insignificant if properly managed. The absence of major incidents in the Swedish nuclear program helps to confirm that view. SKB has continuously produced a series of information booklets to the public about performance, costs, operation, and waste management in the nuclear plants in a fashion that underlines safety and openness.

Within the KBS project the nuclear industry demonstrated the safety of their models by an accumulation of knowledge, which was discussed in an open technical review. General access was facilitated through the publication of important facts and arguments, and the government organized several teams of national and international experts to comment on the generic safety of the suggested method. In all, thirty-seven organizations and twelve experts took part in the revision of the first report, and out of this group an informal international peer group formed that studied the next two reports. Berkhout (1991) describes the evaluation of the technical multibarrier concept as one of excess validation, where the "surplus" over what is needed under ordinary scientific-technical conditions was brought about to satisfy the needs of a social settlement of nuclear disposal.

The scientific acceptance of the KBS method facilitated a pragmatic legislative move; the Parliament changed the wording of the 1977 Stipulation Act by replacing a requirement to show "how and where the absolutely safe disposal of HLW can be done" with one to "show that a method exists for the management and final deposition . . . that can be approved regarding safety and radiation protection." The following siting process of the SFR and CLAB repositories showed that the actual geological structures had some serious potential disadvantages, especially at Forsmark. Yet despite partly unsatisfactory natural conditions, and some local opposition within the commune in which Forsmark is situated, a modified repository construction was implemented. In Sweden, disputes over nuclear waste management have mainly focused on HLW, while the handling of operational wastes has provoked less conflict, but it is tempting to interpret the localization of the SFR repository as a victory for an incremental building of a policy based on institutional consensus and trust in technology, under the restriction of widespread initial social doubt and distrust.

This conclusion is confirmed by the recent appearance of a commune that explicitly expressed a willingness to accommodate the Swedish HLW repository. In Summer 1992, Arjeplog (see Figure 8.1) in the far north invited SKB to perform a tentative siting survey. Arjeplog has long faced a declining population trend, and employment in the dominant mining industry will drop in a few years as crucial mineral deposits are being depleted. Jobs are desperately wanted, and the know-how of miners is suitable for construction and monitoring activities required in an HLW repository. However, there is reason to believe that several local conflicts of interest will appear. The indigenous people, the Sami, who had bad experiences after the Chernobyl accident, are likely to oppose the presence of nuclear wastes in the area, and so are conservationists and the tourist business. Further, risks attached to long overland transports have to be carefully considered. As was mentioned earlier, all Swedish nuclear reactors are located along the coasts of southern Sweden, which has permitted relatively cheap and safe transportation of radioactive matter by a specially equipped vessel.

The same implementation strategy for acceptance will be repeated now on a local scale. Scientific investigations to find "best" solutions are part of the plans, including consensus building by the participation of political parties and local interest groups, and a local referendum. The ultimate local arguments, however, lie in the anticipation of economic prosperity for the area. Funds for final deposition have accumulated, corresponding to 7 percent of the value of the electricity produced, which should guarantee the final feasibility of the project. There is plenty of time for study; final deposition of HLW is not scheduled to start until 2010. Eventually, however, this siting decision will demonstrate a frank trade-off between economic development and environmental concerns in the area. Or—from the harmony perspective of "the Swedish Model" (Milner, 1989)—if accepted, the siting will be a successful compromise, demonstrating how a NIMBY syndrome may develop into an IMBY situation.

NOTES

This work was funded by the Swedish Council for Planning and Coordination of Research (FRN).

1. Acronyms used in this chapter are generally taken from the Swedish.

REFERENCES

Berkhout, Frans. 1991. *Radioactive Waste: Politics and Technology*. London: Routledge.
Holmberg, Sören. 1988. Svenska folkets åsikter om kärnkraft och slutförvaring efter Tjernobyl. (The Swedish people's opinions about nuclear power and final deposition after Chernobyl.) Stockholm: SKN Rapport 30. In Swedish.
———. 1990. Svenska folket riskbedömer kärnkraftens slutförvaring. (The Swedish people assess the risks of nuclear waste deposition.) In Sören Holmberg and Lennart Weibull, eds. *Medier och opinion i Sverige*. SOM-undersökningen 1989. SOM-rapport 5. Göteborg, Sweden: Göteborgs universitet, Department of Political Science. In Swedish.
Kemp, Ray. 1991. Institutional Innovation to Generate the Public Acceptance of Radioactive Waste Disposal. In Lewis Roberts and Albert Weale, eds. *Innovation and Environmental Risk*. London: Belhaven Press.
Kraft, Michael and Bruce Clary. 1991. Citizen Participation and the NIMBY Syndrome; Public Response to Radioactive Waste Disposal. *Western Political Quarterly*, 44, 2:299–318.
Lewin, Leif. 1988. *Ideology and Strategy: A Century of Swedish Politics*. Cambridge: Cambridge University Press.
Lidskog, Rolf and Ingemar Elander. 1990. Beslut och konflikt vid lokalisering av miljöfarligt avfall. (Decision and conflict in the siting of hazardous wastes.) *Statsvetenskaplig Tidskrift*, 3:260–269. In Swedish.

Löwgren, Marianne and Björn Segrell. 1991. Environmental Issues in Sweden 1973–
    1989: Science and Policy. *Environmental Management,* 15, 5:613–622.
Milner, Henry. 1989. *Sweden: Social Democracy in Practice.* Oxford: Oxford University
    Press.
Vedung, Evert. 1979. *Kärnkraften och regeringen Fälldins fall.* (Nuclear power and the
    fall of Fälldin government.) Uppsala: Rabén och Sjögren. In Swedish.
Wittrock, Björn and Stefan Lindström. 1984. *De stora programmens tid—forskning och
    energi i svensk politik.* (The era of big programs—research and energy in Swedish
    politics.) Stockholm: Förlaget Akademilitteratur AB. In Swedish.
Wynne, Brian. 1987. Risk Management and Hazardous Waste. *Implementation and the
    Dialectics of Credibility.* Luxembourg, Luxembourg: IIASA.

9

Subsystem Politics and the Nuclear Weapons Complex: Congressional Oversight of DOE's Environmental Restoration Program

JAMES A. THURBER *and* TIMOTHY C. EVANSON

The focus of this case study is congressional oversight of the U.S. Department of Energy's nuclear weapons complex.[1] The analysis studies the styles of interaction between Congress and the U.S. Department of Energy (DOE), and the variables which cause fluctuations in the patterns of interaction.

Using interviews with congressional, executive branch, and private sector respondents and an analysis of primary source documents, this chapter analyzes the nature of oversight decisionmaking through the lens of subsystems theory (Thurber, 1991). The study concludes that the subsystem which undergirds the complex clean-up process began as a closed, low-profile decisionmaking system in the 1940s through the 1970s and evolved into a more open, conflictual, and competitive system of actors in the 1980s and 1990s.

THEORETICAL CONCEPTS

Explaining Oversight

Oversight is the most common form of interaction between the executive and legislative branches. Broadly defined, "[l]egislative oversight is behavior by legislators and their staffs, individually or collectively, which results in an impact, intended or not, on bureaucratic behavior" (Ogul, 1976:11). The Constitution as well as political reality often forces the two branches to cooperate in this oversight process, but conflict occurs with unsettling regularity.

Why oversight occurs is poorly understood, but political incentives are often cited as reasons why oversight exists and takes the forms it does.

Following Richard Fenno (1973) and David Mayhew (1974), scholars argue that oversight occurs so that representatives will be able to gain prestige within Congress, ensure good public policy, gain electoral advantage, or carry out the wishes of the electorate. However, this does not explain why oversight varies in its substance, in its rate of occurrence, or whether it is pursued by committees or individuals.

Many analyses have focused on the cost of conducting oversight. Matthew McCubbins and Thomas Schwartz (1984) contend that Congress prefers "fire alarm" to "police patrol" oversight to keep costs low. It is also suggested that Congress chooses to require reporting arrangements such as regularly submitted reports, frequent testimony, extensive recordkeeping, and other legal forms to ensure that Congress can review decisions by following the "paper trail" left behind (Fiorina, 1982).

However, the "fire alarm" explanation does not contribute much to oversight theory. The model has several flaws, not the least of which is that it assumes that the executive branch and interested pressure groups will remain unaware that the burden of costs has shifted.[2] More importantly, however, the "fire alarm" model only predicts the form oversight takes. It does not predict the rate at which oversight will occur or whether the hearings will address problems in an informed or substantive manner. Therefore, we must consider whether different political environments create different incentives and whether the variables which impel movement from one environment to the next can be identified.

The theory of subsystem politics models different environments which can affect oversight. Subsystem theory assumes that interest groups acting as functional representatives are the engine of the modern political system.[3] Individual preferences do not matter so much as the aggregate effects they produce.

> The subsystem theory identifies three levels of analysis. These range from: . . . *macropolicy systems* or "high politics" (general policy decision with major political effects involving broad public interests, visibility, divisiveness, extensive media coverage, and many participants) to *policy subsystems* (ranging in turn from dominant to competitive to disintegrated) to *micropolicy systems* (narrowly focused decision making involving a very small, often closed group of decision makers). (Thurber, 1991:320)

Several variables are used to distinguish these systems from one another, the most important of which are the visibility of decisions, the scope of conflict, the level of conflict, and the number of participants in the decisionmaking system (ibid.:321).

Within the policy subsystem category, there exist three subsystems. Dominant subsystems exhibit stable relations among a small group of decisionmakers. Uncertainty and information costs are low, and opportunistic behavior is controlled by the use of norms and clear communication channels. Competitive subsystems exhibit coalitions that are short-lived due to competition for resources and information, while in the disintegrated subsystems the level of conflict and visibility are higher. Large numbers of participants engage the interested public in the disintegrated subsystem.

Importantly, subsystem theory does not consider political conflict to be undesirable.[4] For example, a dominant subsystem (which controls conflict), such as that which is often predominant in Social Security policymaking, may be beneficial, or it may be harmful, as in the case of nuclear weapons facilities, where safety issues seemed to be ignored in favor of increased production until the 1980s.

Explaining Bureaucratic Responsiveness

Subsystem theory does not, however, generally predict agency behavior. A close reading of the history of DOE and its predecessor agencies on the issue of nuclear weapons production makes it clear that agency culture was an important determinant of bureaucratic behavior. However, as the decisionmaking process became more competitive, uncertainty over how to complete the clean-up process and satisfy DOE's critics better explained the agency's actions.

An agency's behavior is often influenced by the agency's culture. Culture influences the definition of goals by creating selective attention to problems, establishing criteria for problem identification and problem solving, and making judgments about which conflicting tasks to perform first (Stinchcombe, 1965; Kimberly, 1975; Kimberly and Niles, 1980).

An agency's culture may provide clues as to how an agency will resist the implementation of a new policy. Since professional ethics and paradigms often form the basis of an agency's culture, it is important to examine the background of an agency's core staff (Pruitt, 1979). Some agencies, such as the Centers for Disease Control, permit only specialized personnel such as medical professionals as staff. When professionally staffed agencies resist policy implementation, they usually engage in three forms of resistance: leaving the agency, voicing complaints internally, and neglecting policy implementation (Hirschman, 1970; Golden, 1992). Certain careers such as law actually train and encourage their practitioners to voice complaints, but others (particularly scientific professions) tend toward professional norms that are less adversarial, making resignation or neglect more likely (Golden, 1992:35). Thus, when job prospects in the private sector are dim, an agency whose workers are primarily drawn from the scientific community will choose neglect as a form of resistance.

Uncertainty over a program's success or basis of support and a lack of resources may also encourage an agency to implement policy poorly. Complex technologies often create uncertainty over whether the task will be successfully completed. In such situations, managers often seek additional resources, or "slack," in order to have enough resources so that failure can be avoided. If these additional resources are not forthcoming, the agency may seek to avoid discretion in the implementation process to avoid being blamed for the failure. As uncertainty, the risk of failure, or political pressures increase, the agency may seek progressively less discretion. Eventually, the agency may abdicate its discretion entirely and essentially force Congress to be the primary decisionmaker (Thompson, 1967:119, 129; Romzek and Dubnick, 1987). The agency's avoidance of discretion may be interpreted by the legislature as poor management and as failure to implement the law.

DECISIONMAKING IN THE NUCLEAR WEAPONS COMPLEX FROM THE LATE 1930s TO THE 1970s[5]

The Late 1930s to 1954

From the late 1930s until approximately 1954, the decisionmaking system which governed the production of defense-related nuclear materials was a micropolitical one (Green, 1982; Mazuzan and Walker, 1984:12, 25–26, 211). Since early research on nuclear physics centered around fission's military applications, the armed services committees in Congress exercised almost exclusive jurisdiction. After the passage of the first Atomic Energy Act in 1948, the Atomic Energy Commission (AEC) exercised this jurisdiction. Within these committees, information about nuclear research and materials was restricted to the chairman, senior minority member, and a few others (Morone and Woodhouse, 1989:45). Hearings on the nuclear weapons complex were often held in executive session, and programs were judged by whether they attained results. In the executive branch, few outside of the president's inner circle knew about the research program under way, and most research prior to 1945 was conducted by the Department of War (renamed the Department of Defense in 1947).

Since little was known about nuclear materials and radiation, few regulations governing storage and wastes existed. This was partly because government officials were unsure about what to regulate, and partly because nuclear materials were produced in very small quantities. Wastes produced by research were stored on-site in drums, a technique considered safe by most scientists.[6] Few environmental or worker safety laws existed at this time, and these laws often did not regulate radioactive waste storage.

The secrecy surrounding nuclear research was tight. This was due to the military nature of nearly all nuclear research and the onset of World War II. However, this veil of secrecy also protected nuclear researchers from public pressure to clean up spills or adopt safety regulations.

The work atmosphere at the nuclear research facilities during the 1930s, 1940s, and 1950s remained focused on the development and production of nuclear weapons for national security purposes. With the Germans, Japanese, Soviets, and Chinese all working on atomic bombs at one time or another, the emphasis seemed justified.

Public opinion did not have much influence over nuclear research and weapons production until after 1954. Environmental groups were often small and had little access to government (Zinberg, 1984). Although unions often emphasized safety, they had no members in the military, physics community, or nuclear materials processing industry. The public was afraid of atomic weapons and nuclear war, but felt the production of such weapons was justified to maintain national security (Rosa and Freudenberg, 1984).

1954 to the 1970s

The micropolitical system that protected nuclear weapons production from scrutiny became a dominant subsystem in 1954. In that year, Congress amended the Atomic Energy Act, making nuclear energy available for civilian uses. New institutions such as the Joint Committee on Atomic Energy (JCAE) in Congress and a reorganized AEC in the executive branch became active in nuclear weapons production politics. The new participants were few in number, however, and older actors appeared to be able to convince them that closed decisionmaking processes and an open exchange of information within the subsystem were in the national interest.

Congressional oversight of the weapons production complex remained relatively unchanged. Oversight was still limited, informal, and focused on production. Weapons production no longer commanded presidential attention, however. Increasingly, individuals with working knowledge about weapons production (and its problems) worked in the Department of Defense (DOD) or for contractors connected with the program.

Few new laws and regulations governing weapons production were created during this period. Knowledge about the effects of radiation was limited almost exclusively to the effects of exposure to atomic weapons tests on soldiers. Few in the medical, physics, or military communities knew how radioactive contamination spread, how fast it spread, what storage devices could contain radiation, how long radioactive contamination took to manifest itself, what effects low-level or high-level exposure to radiation had over time, or how to clean up soil or aquifers contaminated by radioactive pollution. What regulations did exist often did not apply to defense facilities.

With secrecy still tight and few outside the weapons production subsystem aware of what went on inside DOD and AEC weapons plants, little pressure to deal with safety problems existed. Absent this pressure, executive branch officials and JCAE and armed services committee members faced few incentives to question the focus on weapons production. The high level of secrecy and the growing political isolation of "bomb makers" within the physics community also prevented information about new safety precautions from filtering into the weapons production complex. This division largely ensured that for four decades to come, safety measures in the complex essentially remained frozen at 1950s levels.

The culture of the weapons production community remained fixated on production, but began to emphasize an engineering approach ("Watkins Confirmed," 1989:2336). This new cultural trait within the weapons production community had been added by the influx of civilian engineers created by the civilian nuclear energy program. The "engineering culture" emphasized the use of rational thought, principles of engineering, and a value-free or apolitical style of decisionmaking (Mazuzan and Walker, 1984:68–69). Problems were often recognized only if they interfered with weapons design or production, and the solutions discussed were likely to be engineering solutions. Thus, many in the weapons production complex were oblivious to the health and environmental effects of their work.

SOURCES OF CHANGE IN NUCLEAR WEAPONS PRODUCTION DECISIONMAKING

The changes which led the nuclear weapons complex subsystem to become competitive in the 1980s can be traced to several factors and events in the 1970s. Although some of these factors only indirectly contributed to the shift away from the dominant subsystem, the "ripple effect" they produced was important.

Growing public distress over environmental and safety issues often led to the enactment of federal legislation, and these laws permitted more openness in the subsystem. These measures initially exempted the nuclear weapons production facilities from scrutiny. However, court decisions, federal legislation, and state and local actions during the 1970s chipped away at the sovereign immunity and exemptions enjoyed by the nuclear weapons complex (Zinberg, 1984:238; Rosa and Freudenberg, 1984:20). Soon the facilities were exposed to environmental and safety regulations, and problems at the plants became known.

In 1974, the AEC was abolished. For a large segment of the public and for many in Congress, the AEC's duty to promote civilian nuclear power had clearly interfered with the agency's duty to regulate the industry. So, in the wake of the first OPEC oil embargo, the AEC was divided into two new agencies.Its regulatory duties were given to the newly created Nuclear Regulatory Commission (NRC), and its responsibility to promote nuclear energy was transferred to the Energy Research and Development Administration (ERDA). DOD became the agency responsible for the design and testing of atomic weapons.

Following reform recommendations in the Senate, the JCAE was abolished in 1976 and its jurisdiction redistributed, permitting new participants who did not share in the goals and norms of the dominant subsystem to enter the decisionmaking process (Temples, 1980:249). Many of the new participants were electorally motivated to uncover and publicize problems at the weapons plants. As norms of behavior broke down and conflict over goals grew, communication became less open and the subsystem weakened.

The accidents at Three Mile Island in 1979 and Chernobyl in 1986 interacted with the increase in the production of nuclear warheads under the Reagan administration to destroy the dominant subsystem. The two nuclear accidents mobilized a large, vocal, nationally based constituency that pressured Congress to ensure the safety of nuclear power plants, research centers, and weapons production facilities. This concern increased as the administration accelerated production of atomic warheads. Soon conservative members of Congress were investigating the atomic weapons plants to identify problems and seeking to fix them before the problems became political liabilities. Liberals also sought to expose problems at the plants in order to justify a shutdown in nuclear weapons production. These investigations soon uncovered even more safety and environmental problems.

The increase in congressional activity can be seen in even the roughest measures of oversight activity. Figures 9.1 and 9.2 show an increasing trend in the total number of hearings and total number of witnesses heard by Congress during the 1980s. Hearings became more frequent, and more were held during each year and quarter, indicating that Congress was abandoning its irregular approach to oversight. The large increase in hearings held in 1983 is probably due to the interest in nuclear waste issues created by the passage of the Nuclear Waste Policy Act (NWPA) of 1982. But even more importantly, the number of expert and executive branch witnesses appearing at each hearing shows a definable upward trend after the Chernobyl accident in 1986. This suggests that oversight hearings were more substantive in the competitive subsystem. The rise in the number of hearings and witnesses after 1986 also supports the proposition that Congress had abandoned production as the weapons complex's sole goal, and was actively considering other missions for DOE.

Increased public awareness of waste issues, as reflected in the number of popular newspaper and magazine articles about this subject, also occurred. Figure 9.3 shows dramatic increases in the number of articles published after the Chernobyl accident in 1986. Although the effect of the increase on the national public conscience probably was not great, the effect was pronounced where nuclear weapons production plants were located.[7] This localized effect contributed to the pressure on Congress and may have led to more congressional inquiries.

CONGRESSIONAL–EXECUTIVE INTERACTION IN THE COMPETITIVE SUBSYSTEM OF THE 1980s

Reorganizing DOE and Completing the Five-Year Plan

During the 1980s, Congress, DOE, and other political actors repeatedly clashed over the purpose and management of the nuclear weapons complex. Although a majority in Congress believed that the emphasis on production should give way to safety and environmental issues, the coalitional nature of the subsystem encouraged behavior that did not make agreement easy.

During this period, DOE seemed to resist attempts to switch the agency's emphasis from production to environmental restoration. However, Congress mandated that DOE develop a clean-up plan in the 1982 NWPA. DOE subsequently issued the Defense Waste Management Plan in 1983. This plan called for the construction of waste treatment and disposal facilities, the construction of new storage facilities, and a safer

Figure 9.1
Number of Congressional Hearings on the DOE Weapons Complex Clean-Up, by Quarter, 1980–1990

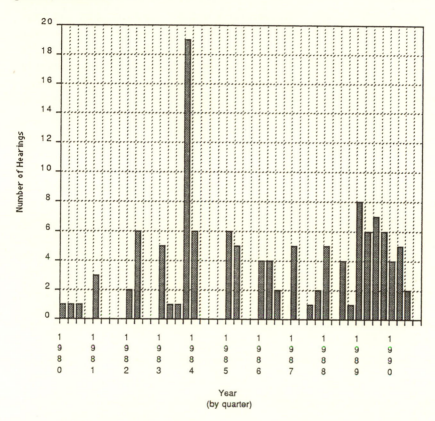

transportation system for nuclear waste. As constituent pressure to clean up the weapons plants built throughout this period, Congress intensified its oversight of DOE's weapons program (see Figure 9.1). In these hearings, Congress pressured DOE to provide more details about its environmental restoration program, but congressional efforts were stymied by high turnover among top DOE personnel. DOE did not appear to actively address Congress's complaints until Admiral James D. Watkins became the secretary of energy in March 1989.

Secretary Watkins immediately restructured DOE to enable it to better manage its facilities by integrating waste management and environmental clean-up activities under a single office. Established November 1, 1989, the Office of Environmental Restoration and Waste Management consolidated programs previously implemented by offices with other major responsibilities—primarily the Defense Programs office, the Nuclear En-

Figure 9.2
Number of Witnesses at Congressional Hearings on the DOE Weapons Complex
Clean-Up, by Quarter, 1980–1990

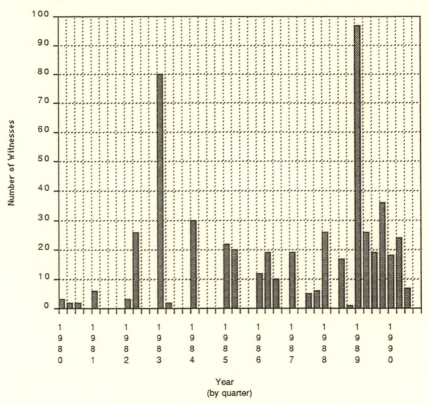

ergy office, and the Office of Energy Research. Watkins also ordered the
completion of a long-delayed, congressionally mandated five-year plan.
Issued in August 1989, the Environmental Restoration and Waste Management: Five-Year Plan, Fiscal Years 1992–1996 (or Five-Year Plan) incorporated much of the 1983 Defense Waste Management Plan and specified
that DOE achieve compliance with all environmental requirements within
thirty years. Watkins's goal was to use the Five-Year Plan to restore DOE's
credibility with Congress, the public, and the states.

Watkins's reorientation also included policy changes. Watkins required
stricter environmental compliance by contractors (which operate virtually all
DOE facilities) and ordered the Office of Environmental Restoration and
Waste Management to implement the plan. Under pressure from and with the
consent of several congressional committees, Watkins also reorganized
DOE's environmental programs around three major activities: environmental

Figure 9.3
Number of Popular Articles in Newspapers and Magazines on the DOE Weapons Complex Clean-Up, by Quarter, 1980–1990

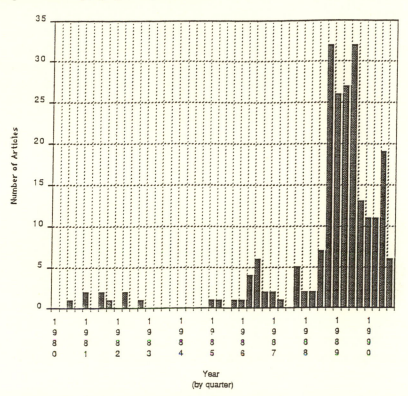

Year
(by quarter)

Source: New York Times Index, Washington Post Index, and *Reader's Guide to Periodical Literature.* Articles which refer generally to health, safety, or nuclear materials production issues or to technical or scientific issues were not counted. Key words used included: for the *Times Index,* atomic weapons and radioactive waste disposal; for the *Post Index,* radioactive waste disposal and atomic (or nuclear) weapons; and for the *Reader's Guide,* atomic (or nuclear) bombs-manufacture, radioactive waste disposal, and United States Department of Energy. Key words differ because different indexes may use different rubrics as subject headings; however, key words used here are comparable. Also, an index may use different key words for the same subject over time, or use many key words to cover one subject.

restoration, corrective activities, and waste management. To fund this plan, Watkins asked for and received increased funding. Appropriations rose from $1.3 billion in fiscal year (FY) 1989 to $3.8 billion in FY 1991, with a request for nearly $4.3 billion in FY 1992. The total estimated DOE weapons clean-up budget for FY 1991 to FY 1996 topped $30 billion.

However, the Five-Year Plan lacked detail. Despite repeated congressional requests, Secretary Watkins and DOE were not forthcoming with much additional information. Congress soon demanded that the annual updates to the Five-Year Plan include more details, but the revised Five-Year Plan issued in June 1990 still lacked many of the changes Congress wanted.

Congressional concern over the Five-Year Plan stemmed from the fact that although the plans were supposed to help Congress set budget priorities for FY 1992 through FY 1996, they lacked the details essential to permit budgetary prioritization. Congress became concerned that the nuclear weapons complex environmental restoration program would balloon in cost and become worrisomely inefficient and ineffective if DOE did not do more to assess its funding needs itself. Because of these problems, the thirty-year cost estimates (such as the widely cited $155 billion figure) are highly speculative, and DOE is no longer attempting to estimate costs.

Prioritization Problems

The most difficult technical problems at DOE weapons production facilities involve waste generated or stored prior to 1970. The composition and location of this pre-1970 waste is unknown, however. In addition, most of the pre-1970 waste has been buried with nonradioactive, chemically hazardous substances. DOE has hesitated to conduct studies of these contamination problems largely because it fears the repercussions that would come if the studies showed that contamination at weapons sites was more widespread than estimated.

However, Congress pressed DOE to undertake some preliminary steps, and DOE responded positively. In June 1989, Watkins announced a ten-point plan which included: the establishment of "tiger teams" to examine sites for possible contamination; provisions to make environmental responsibilities for program managers more distinct; increased incentives for environmental compliance; and greater environmental funding proposals.

However, DOE has failed to prioritize its contamination activities or the contaminated sites. DOE's approach is to identify environmental problems, place them into four categories denoting relative risk to the public, and then integrate environmental degradation factors into the analysis. The degree of uncertainty with the risk-based ranking in each instance is also categorized.[8] This system has been criticized on the grounds that it is too data-intensive, cannot distinguish short-term from long-term risks, cannot identify the most-exposed individuals, and conflicts with legal obligations. Additionally, constituents in districts where weapons plants are located have pressured their representatives to abandon DOE's ranking system so that their site gets cleaned up first. DOE, however, has thus far resisted congressional attempts to change the ranking system. DOE's resistance, however, has resulted in additional conflict between the agency and Congress.

The clean-up effort has also been stymied because DOE must often negotiate with other political actors. DOE has often been forced to enter into interagency agreements (IAs) with the Environmental Protection Agency (EPA) and various states in order to meet others' regulatory standards. However, fulfilling the terms of the compliance agreements is expected to require steady increases in clean-up funding, which could eventually conflict with budget limitations. According to most of the respondents interviewed for this study, it is not clear whether a lack of congressional appropriations would protect DOE from enforcement action over missed clean-up deadlines or not.[9]

Controversy Over Long-Term Storage and Decommissioning Policies

DOE plans to convert high-level nuclear waste (HLW) into glasslike forms and dispose of it in an underground geologic repository known as the Waste Isolation Pilot Plant (WIPP). Construction began on this repository in New Mexico in the early 1970s. But controversy surrounds DOE's storage plans. Geologic problems at the WIPP site have led some to conclude that DOE rushed certification of the site in order to present the agency's critics with a *fait accompli* before site selection could be halted.

Additionally, the state of New Mexico abandoned its pro-WIPP stand of the late 1970s, and no longer wants WIPP. In an apparent attempt to stop the project, New Mexico is refusing to issue the licenses and permits that would allow the site to open. WIPP was designed to hold defense nuclear waste generated between 1970 and 2015, but neither DOE nor Congress has decided whether the large quantities of pre-1970 waste should also be stored at WIPP. Finally, to the extent that any nuclear waste is mixed with hazardous materials, the management of that waste is subject to regulation by EPA under the Resource Conservation and Recovery Act (RCRA). All storage facilities for mixed wastes, therefore, will have to obtain permits under RCRA as well, and DOE believes this will cause long delays in the WIPP project.

DOE recently tried to force a decision about what to do about the long-term storage of defense nuclear waste. Under pressure from DOE, the Bureau of Land Management (BLM) agreed in January 1991 to permit DOE to use land set aside for WIPP for radioactive waste storage. Without EPA approval, DOE shipped approximately 4,500 barrels of waste to WIPP in September 1991, despite complaints from Congress, the state of New Mexico, EPA, the Nuclear Regulatory Commission, and the Department of the Interior. RCRA lawsuits were filed by New Mexico and several environmental groups. In January 1992, the U.S. District Court for the District of Columbia ruled that BLM's land-use order was illegal, and DOE was permanently enjoined from storing any more waste at WIPP until Congress legislatively affirmed such activity.[10]

CONCLUSION

Subsystem theory provides a hierarchy of decisionmaking processes that enables us to make sense of U.S. pluralism. By focusing on the visibility of decisions, the scope of conflict, the level of conflict, and the number of participants, subsystem theory creates a model which is dynamic and does not view conflict as dysfunctional.

In our case study, DOE repeatedly seems to neglect implementation of the environmental restoration program, but seems to do so for reasons that vary considerably over time. Initially, DOE's apparent neglect of the implementation process seems to reflect a cultural resistance to the new policy of environmental restoration. Turnover at DOE was high and the agency put off release of the first Five-Year Plan. Soon, however, resistance seemed to weaken. Secretary Watkins's confirmation and the decrease in personnel turnover after 1989 signaled the end of the policy resistance stage.

Competitive behavior among subsystem actors then seems to quickly become evident. Secretary Watkins used the first Five-Year Plan to build a supportive coalition in Congress, and he was successful enough to be rewarded with large funding increases.

However, it appears as if DOE did not rely on coalition building for long. As uncertainty over the size of the contamination problem grew and public criticism of DOE increased, DOE seemed to shift its implementation strategy. Watkins revised contractor performance standards, told Congress that DOE would shift budget priorities dramatically in future budgets, and reorganized the department twice.

It is important, however, to understand that the coalition DOE appeared to build after 1989 was not a cooperative one, for DOE sought to protect itself from its critics by inducing Congress to dominate the agency's decisionmaking. To maneuver itself into this position, DOE appears to

have neglected policy implementation. Reports were not detailed or released on time, and priorities were not set. DOE refused to estimate budget
needs itself, and denied Congress access to information. This neglect
consequently seems to have forced Congress to accept political responsibility for the environmental restoration program. Inducing Congress to
take responsibility for decisions that might draw heavy political fire
seemed to be a sound strategy for an agency that felt it could not survive
in a competitive political system.

Uncertainty was also reduced through judicial action. Uncertainty over
support for the environmental restoration program and the likelihood of
the program's success encouraged DOE to neglect implementation. This
neglect prompted DOE's critics to sue the agency for noncompliance with
the law. However, the ultimate result of a court decision, whether adverse
or not, would be to reduce uncertainty surrounding the clean-up program's
goals, basis of support, and implementation. DOE's precipitate action at
the WIPP site in 1991 can be readily explained in this light.

The subsystem model used to study the politics of defense nuclear
waste accurately described changes in oversight in this policy area.
Conflict and coalitional behavior were often the primary motivation for
increases in the frequency of oversight. As the political costs of trying
to "keep the problem quiet" rose, the benefits that holding hearings
delivered increased and more hearings were held, and oversight hearings became more substantive.

Although the subsystem model was useful in understanding the politics
that govern defense nuclear waste, it is not clear that controversy and
conflict in the subsystem has ended. Congress may attempt to limit DOE's
discretion in administering the program if the agency does not address
congressional concerns or if the budget for environmental restoration must
tighten in response to other budgetary priorities. Various interest groups
not necessarily part of the subsystem may also use the judicial system to
gain access to decisionmaking processes. However, it appears as if DOE
will continue to build supportive coalitions for itself within Congress, and
competition for the resources necessary to control policymaking concerning the defense nuclear weapons complex will continue.

NOTES

1. The DOE weapons complex is divided into four major activities, as follows: (1)
research and development at Los Alamos and Sandia National Laboratories in New
Mexico and Lawrence Livermore National Laboratory in California; (2) nuclear materials
production and processing (plutonium and tritium) at the Hanford Plant in Washington

State and the Savannah River Site in South Carolina, along with uranium processing at the Feed Materials Production Center in Ohio and the Idaho National Engineering Laboratory; (3) warhead component production at the Rocky Flats Plant in Colorado, the Y–12 Plant in Tennessee, the Mound Plant in Ohio, the Pinellas Plant in Florida, the Kansas City Plant in Missouri, and the Pantex Plant in Texas for final assembly; and (4) warhead testing at the Nevada Test Site.

2. See James Wilson's (1989:244–251, 246n) discussion of these and other problems. Agencies also often tie unpopular decisions to popular ones (the Navy's "home porting" scheme created public support for the 600-ship Navy, an otherwise unpopular policy in Congress), short-circuiting the "fire alarm" system. See also Joel Aberbach's (1987) claim that congressional staff engage in police patrol oversight in order to achieve their own career goals.

3. Functional representation is defined by James Thurber (1991:326) as "the representation of societal functions through governmental institutions [stemming] from the division of labor and development of expertise and specialization in society."

4. More commonly conflict is seen as dangerous and disruptive; a recent example is the report *Beyond Distrust: Building Bridges Between Congress and the Executive* (Washington, DC: National Academy of Public Administration, 1992).

5. The following history is deeply indebted to works on atomic weapons research and design by Robert Williams and Philip Cantelon (1984) and Fred Kaplan (1983).

6. See AEC staff paper 180/5 AEC/NRC (March 30, 1956). During the 1959 radioactive waste hearings, the AEC reaffirmed this position repeatedly (Mazuzan and Walker, 1984:chap. 12).

7. Allan Mazur (1984) finds evidence that the media have substantially affected public opinion concerning nuclear energy and radioactive waste.

8. The system is called the Multimedia Environmental Pollutant System (MEPS).

9. Until the 1980s DOE interpreted the Atomic Energy Act to mean that it was not subject to outside regulation. Several court decisions have held otherwise; see *Environmental Assistance Foundation v. Hodel*, 586 F.Supp. 1163 (1984). And although no court has ruled specifically on the issue of nuclear waste compliance agreements, the courts have consistently ruled in other cases that a lack of funding does not absolve an agency from fulfilling its responsibilities under the law; see *Wyatt v. Stickney*, 325 F.Supp. 781, 334 F.Supp. 1341 (1971) and 344 F.Supp. 373, 344 F.Supp. 387, 503 F2d 1305 (1972); and *Missouri v. Jenkins*, 110 S.Ct. 1651 (1989).

10. *State of New Mexico et al. v. Watkins*, Civil Action No. 91–2527, 1992 U.S. Dist. LEXIS 981 (Dist. D.C. 1992).

REFERENCES

Aberbach, Joel D. 1987. The Congressional Committee Intelligence System: Information, Oversight, and Change. *Congress and the Presidency*, 14 (Spring):51–76.

Fenno, Richard. 1973. *Congressmen in Committee*. Boston: Little, Brown.

Fiorina, Morris. 1982. Legislative Choice of Regulatory Forms: Legal Process or Administrative Process? *Public Choice*, 39, 1:33–36.

Golden, Marissa M. 1992. Exit, Voice, Loyalty and Neglect: Bureaucratic Responses to Presidential Control During the Reagan Administration. *Journal of Public Administration Research and Theory*, 2 (January):28–62.

Green, Harold. 1982. The Peculiar Politics of Nuclear Power. *Bulletin of the Atomic Scientists*, 38 (December):59–62.

Hirschman, Albert O. 1970. *Exit, Voice and Loyalty: Responses to Decline in Firms, Organizations and States*. Cambridge, MA: Harvard University Press.

Holt, Mark. 1990. *Nuclear Weapons Production Complex: Environmental Compliance and Waste Management*. Washington, DC: Congressional Research Service.

Kaplan, Fred M. 1983. *The Wizards of Armageddon*. New York: Simon and Schuster.

Kimberly, John R. 1975. Environmental Constraints and Organization Structure. *Administrative Science Quarterly*, 20 (March):1–9.

Kimberly, John R. and Robert H. Niles, eds. 1980. *Organizational Life Cycle*. San Francisco: Jossey-Bass.

Luoma, Jon R. 1989. U.S. Turning To New Technologies To Clean Up Arms Plants. *New York Times*, January 3, p. C1.

Mayhew, David. 1974. *Congress: The Electoral Connection*. New Haven, CT: Yale University Press.

Mazur, Allan. 1984. Media Influences on Public Attitudes Toward Nuclear Power. In William R. Freudenburg and Eugene A. Rosa, eds. *Public Reaction to Nuclear Power*. Boulder, CO: Westview Press.

Mazuzan, George T. and Samuel J. Walker. 1984. *Controlling the Atom: The Beginnings of Nuclear Regulation, 1946–62*. Berkeley, CA: University of California Press.

McCubbins, Matthew and Thomas Schwartz. 1984. Congressional Oversight Overlooked: Police Patrols versus Fire Alarms. *American Journal of Political Science*, 28 (February):164–179.

Morone, Joseph G. and Edward G. Woodhouse. 1989. *The Demise of Nuclear Energy?* New Haven, CT: Yale University Press.

Ogul, Morris S. 1976. *Congress Oversees the Bureaucracy: Studies in Legislative Supervision*. Pittsburgh: University of Pittsburgh Press.

Pruitt, Charles. 1979. People Doing What they Do Best: Professional Engineers and NHTSA. *Public Administration Review*, 29 (July/August):363–371.

Romzek, Barbara and Mel Dubnick. 1987. Accountability in the Public Sector: Lessons from the Challenger Tragedy. *Public Administration Review*, 47 (May/June):227–238.

Rosa, Eugene A. and William R. Freudenburg. 1984. Nuclear Power at the Crossroads. In William R. Freudenburg and Eugene A. Rosa, eds. *Public Reaction to Nuclear Power*. Boulder, CO: Westview Press.

Schneider, Keith. 1990. Cost of Cleanup at Nuclear Sites is Raised 50%. *New York Times*, July 4, p. A1.

Smith, Jeffrey. 1990. Two U.S. Agencies Sign Agreement on Cleanup of Ohio Uranium Facility. *Washington Post*, April 11, p. A8.

Stinchcombe, Arthur. 1965. Social Structure and Organizations. In James G. March, ed. *Handbook of Organizations*. Chicago: Rand McNally.

Temples, J. 1980. The Politics of Nuclear Power: A Subgovernment in Transition. *Political Science Quarterly*, 95 (Spring):239–260.

Thompson, James D. 1967. *Organizations in Action*. New York: McGraw-Hill.

Thurber, James A. 1991. Dynamics of Policy Subsystems in American Politics. In Allan J. Cigler and Burdett A. Loomis, eds. *Interest Group Politics*. 3rd ed. Washington, DC: Congressional Quarterly Press.

U.S. Congress. Office of Technology Assessment. 1991. *Complex Cleanup: The Environmental Legacy of Nuclear Weapons Production, Summary.* Washington, DC: Office of Technology Assessment.

U.S. Department of Energy. 1990. *Environmental Restoration and Waste Management: Five-Year Plan, Fiscal Years 1992–1996.* Washington, DC: U.S. Department of Energy.

Watkins Confirmed as Energy Secretary, Vows to Change "Culture" of Energy Department. 1989. *Environment Reporter*, 19 (March 3):2336.

Williams, Robert and Philip Cantelon. 1984. *The American Atom.* Philadelphia: University of Pennsylvania Press.

Wilson, James Q. 1989. *Bureaucracy: What Government Agencies Do and Why They Do It.* New York: Basic Books.

Zinberg, Dorothy S. 1984. Public Participation in Nuclear Waste Management Policy: A Brief Historical Overview. In William R. Freudenburg and Eugene A. Rosa, eds. *Public Reaction to Nuclear Power.* Boulder, CO: Westview Press.

10

Environmental Policymaking Under New Federalism: The Hanford Clean-Up

MARCY JEAN EVEREST

Environmental problems in the United States have been troubling policy-makers for two decades. One of the biggest problems is the handling of stored nuclear waste, which has been piling up at commercial reactors and federal weapons facilities for forty-five years. Complicating matters even more is the often extensive site contamination that has occurred with the mismanagement of stored and disposed nuclear waste. The complexities and dangers posed by the handling of such waste have presented a unique challenge to policymakers, who have had to develop and implement waste management and clean-up policies in the midst of constantly changing technology.

These technical challenges were added to the problem of federal agency proliferation in the 1970s, when multiple agencies shared jurisdiction over policy areas. The policy fragmentation which resulted promoted redundant actions of agencies, and policy lacked coordination and direction. The result was environmental policy that has been largely ineffective and unsatisfactory.

The adoption of "New Federalism" in the 1980s has changed that policymaking process. By devolving authority from the federal system to the states, the role of the federal agencies that once dominated the policy-making agenda has been reduced (Davis and Lester, 1989). Individual states must now take the lead in environmental policy development and implementation and are facing the challenge of how to do it more success-fully than the federally dominated system of the past. These rapidly changing circumstances provide a new challenge to our understanding of policy formation and implementation and demand further refinement of existing theories.

In order for states to adjust to this new system and meet the growing public demand for more effective environmental policy, it is necessary to (1) determine the conditions under which policy decisions are now made, (2) evaluate existing models that outline the requirements for successful implementation of policy, and (3) compare those models to existing successful policy programs.

CONDITIONS OF ENVIRONMENTAL POLICYMAKING

The New Federalism pursued by the Reagan administration and adopted over the past decade has fundamentally changed many areas of public policy formation and implementation. The federal government has systematically sought to return the responsibility of public policy to the states by eliminating many federal regulations and reporting practices, terminating federal programs, and increasing block grants for social services which are now managed at the state level. Paralleling the reduced role of the federal government in policy formation and implementation has been a reduction of supporting federal funds. Consequently, the additional management and fiscal responsibilities have increased the demand upon the institutional capacity of state administrations and their available revenues (Gittell, 1986).

A MODEL FOR PREDICTING SUCCESS

The challenge to states has been to find a way to successfully integrate their agencies with federal agencies by developing compatible working relationships in order to maximize the advantages of New Federalism and minimize its disadvantages. Charles Davis and James Lester (1989) have structured a typology (Figure 10.1) that predicts a state's ability to successfully form and implement environmental policy under these circumstances. The typology is based upon the values of two variables: (1) a state's institutional capability of administering policy programs, and (2) a state's dependence upon federal funds to carry out such programs. The value of each variable held by a state places it in one of four categories: interdependence, dependence, independence, and passivity.

To determine the level of dependency or the degree of institutional capacity for each state, Davis and Lester (1989) developed several indicators that measure overall system capacity, such as political support, financial support, administrative support, severity of pollution, related state laws, and past response to environmental problems. If this typology is to prove useful, the evaluation of a state's financial dependency and institu-

Figure 10.1
Typology of State Policy Implementation

		State Institutional Capacity	
State		High	Low
Dependency	High	INTERDEPENDENCE	DEPENDENCE
on Federal			
Aid	Low	INDEPENDENCE	PASSIVITY

tional capacity should predict its ability to respond to the challenges of New Federalism.

In addition to these two variables, related factors also considered important by Davis and Lester in determining the likely success of a state's environmental policy implementation must be examined. These factors influence the need for additional institutional capacity or the importance of funding dependency and include the scope of the problem, interagency cooperation, citizen participation, and political support. This chapter will also examine the additional factor of "agency credibility" and how it relates to a state's ability to successfully implement long-term environmental programs which are required for most nuclear waste clean-up and storage problems. Although it is not included in the original typology, the reason for the inclusion of agency credibility here will be made apparent.

To test whether the theory presented by Davis and Lester accurately predicts a state's capacity, it can be applied to an existing policy program operating under the conditions of New Federalism. This can be done by applying the model to a state currently in the midst of developing and implementing a complex environmental policy program. However, it is important to note that such an application will test only one cell of the typology. For the purposes of this study, the model was applied to the state of Washington and its hazardous and nuclear waste clean-up policy for the Hanford Nuclear Reservation.

APPLYING THEORY TO REALITY

Using their data, Davis and Lester (1989) have classified the state of Washington as "interdependent." That is to say, one would expect to find a high degree of institutional capacity within Washington's state agencies and a high degree of dependence upon federal funds for program implementation. They (1987) also contend that states in this position will find it difficult if not impossible to replace lost federal dollars and have, in fact, found this to be the case. The resulting pressure to replace federal funds, known as "federal stress," is one of the biggest obstacles states have to overcome (Barilleaux, 1988). One such state where environmental policy programs have achieved specified goals in spite of the constraints common to New Federalism is Washington.

The Tri-Party Agreement

To discover how well the model represents the dynamics of an actual policy program, the typology was applied to Washington State's Department of Ecology and the Tri-Party Agreement. The agreement teams the U.S. Department of Energy (DOE), the U.S. Environmental Protection Agency (EPA), and the state of Washington's Department of Ecology (Ecology) in the clean-up effort of the Hanford Reservation in southeast Washington State. The agreement, signed in May 1989, provides a thirty-year blueprint for one of the largest and most expensive hazardous and nuclear waste clean-up projects in the world.

The road to the agreement began in 1984 when Roger Stanley, program manager for the Nuclear and Mixed Waste Program at Ecology, began asking questions of personnel at Hanford regarding waste handling procedures at the facility. According to Tim Nord, project manager for Ecology's Hanford section, "one thing lead to another" and Stanley's questions led to a joint inspection of the Hanford facility by Ecology and the EPA in 1985. During that inspection, numerous violations in procedure were identified and the state of Washington levied a $49,000 fine against the DOE. In 1986 the DOE filed suit against Washington claiming sovereign immunity from Ecology's regulatory authority.

At approximately the same time, the Superfund Amendment Reauthorization Act (SARA) of 1986 was passed, making clean-up of federal nuclear weapons facilities one of the DOE's primary mandates. This act brought the DOE to the bargaining table, and negotiations on the Tri-Party Agreement began in 1988. Although the decision that levied the fine against the DOE was eventually overturned, it has not pursued further regulatory relief from Ecology and the EPA in the courts. According to Nord, SARA and subsequent legislation have bolstered Ecology's legal standing regarding regulatory authority, and future court decisions were expected to favor Ecology.

The Scope of the Problem

In order to appreciate the significance of the Tri-Party Agreement, it is important to first understand the scope of the environmental problem at

Hanford. The original mission of the Hanford Works, built in 1943 by the Army Corps of Engineers and the DuPont Corporation, was to supply weapons-grade plutonium for the Manhattan Project. The site began with three plutonium-producing reactors and expanded to nine in 1964. By 1971 all but one were shut down. In 1988, the Senate Armed Services Committee recommended cutting all funds for the continued operation of the remaining N-Reactor at Hanford and it, too, was shut down.

Throughout four decades of plutonium production the disposal of hazardous and nuclear waste products was handled in a number of different ways. Waste was dumped into the soil, released into the air, or held in storage tanks located only a few miles from the banks of the Columbia River. Evidence gathered by the EPA indicates that more than 100 million gallons of toxic liquid waste were dumped into the ground at Hanford during the 1940s and 1950s, and it is conservatively estimated that 750,000 gallons of high-level nuclear waste has leaked from a number of single-shell storage tanks located at the site (Steele, 1991). In all, the liquid discharges have raised the water table in certain areas under the reservation as much as 75 feet and contaminated at least 120 square miles of ground water (Steele, 1991).

Much of the waste was dumped into underground drain systems that used the soil as a filter. This system was designed to dispose of waste overflow when tanks were full and storage space was limited and could not accommodate all of the waste material. Among the many radioactive toxins that were dumped was technetium 99, which has a half life of 212,000 years, and iodine 129, which has a half life of approximately 16 million years. It is also estimated that up to 580,000 gallons of carbon tetrachloride was dumped into the soil and has now contaminated more than seven square miles of ground water. All three are known carcinogens (Wald, 1991).

Official information regarding the extent of the contamination at Hanford was finally released to Ecology and the public in 1986 as the DOE reluctantly declassified documents concerning past facility operations. This official admission followed years of public protest over facility operations, and citizen demand that the site be cleaned up and the extent of damage and risk to health and the environment be determined. Although most of the public criticism had been leveled against the DOE and the operating contractors at Hanford, it was Ecology that aggressively began pursuing a policy solution that would respond to public demands. In order to fulfill that policy goal and bring about a meaningful clean-up project, the state of Washington had to find money, and lots of it (Nord int., 1991).

Securing Federal Funding Resources

According to Davis and Lester (1989), the degree that a state is dependent upon federal funds for the implementation of environmental programs can influence a state's ability to maintain or execute such programs. It is obvious that Washington could not afford to fund a clean-up effort of the magnitude required for Hanford and that federal funds would be needed to attempt such a project. (The estimated cost now exceeds $50 billion.) As the pressure of fiscal stress continues, states at the mercy of federal funding will likely find federal support continually decreasing (Davis and Lester, 1987). These conditions would initially appear to put the clean-up program at Hanford in considerable jeopardy. However, in 1986 SARA added Section 120 to the Comprehensive Environmental Response, Compensation, and Liability Act (CERCLA) of 1980. This amendment mandates that the federal agency responsible for contamination of the environment provide the funds for clean-up. This legally bound the DOE to pursue financing for the clean-up program through its own budget process. In addition, CERCLA mandated that the EPA evaluate hazardous waste sites across the country and create a National Priority List (NPL) to designate the country's most critical clean-up needs. Portions of the Hanford Reservation were on that list. From the beginning of the agreement negotiation process, the state was aware of the legal and political implications of CERCLA and SARA and used them to "encourage" the DOE's cooperation (Nord int., 1991).

In addition, the Tri-Party Agreement incorporates "enforceable" milestones into the language of the contract. This means that the DOE must provide the funds necessary to meet those agreed-upon goals or be subject to legal action by the state of Washington. Any changes in the proposed costs of the procedures designed to meet the milestones must be agreed upon by all three agencies and the schedule for each milestone must be strictly observed. Both Ecology and the EPA have approached such change requests by the DOE with extreme "caution," as they recognize that the DOE's interests and national priorities may conflict with the priorities of the agreement (Sherwood int., 1991). Without the stringent funding language of the agreement, it is doubtful that the DOE's financial commitment to Hanford would be as generous. By using existing law and incorporating enforceable milestones into the contract language, Ecology has to this point successfully guaranteed adequate access to federal funds to meet the needs of the program.

Adequate Institutional Capacity

According to Davis and Lester (1989), a state's "institutional capacity to absorb decentralized programs" is a primary influence upon successful implementation of environmental policy. Institutional capacity is described as the "political, fiscal, and managerial" ability of public officials to "develop and administer public policies." Those public officials must possess adequate levels of institutional capacity in order to successfully implement policies. As administrative responsibilities for states have increased with New Federalism, state agencies have been expanded and in some cases restructured.

Such is the case with the state of Washington. When SARA put the authority for clean-up policy in the hands of the state and CERCLA required that the DOE pay for the clean-up program, Ecology had to expand its institutional capacity. In 1984, the Hanford section of Ecology had a two-person staff and a $125,000 budget. To meet the needs of the Tri-Party Agreement's oversight and administrative functions the department expanded in personnel and funding. Today, the staff size has increased to fifty-two and the budget to $5 million (Nord int., 1991).

Clearly, the ability of a state to meet the challenges of an integrated, comprehensive policy program may also be hindered if the scope of the environmental problem addressed is large and difficult to physically contain, or when the scope of the problem is so large that it overwhelms the technical resources of a state (Davis and Lester, 1989). Problems that are large in scope, like those at Hanford, can often only be ameliorated with extensive federal resources. With over a thousand designated clean-up sites on the reservation and a multitude of complex technical challenges, only the DOE had the required number of technically trained staff needed to implement the clean-up project. The Tri-Party Agreement acknowledged this fact by employing the DOE and the 15,000-plus Hanford staff through the clean-up contract. This action has assured an adequate supply of trained personnel, not to mention the general good will that continued employment of facility staff has produced in the local communities.

Creating Successful Interagency Cooperation

According to Davis and Lester (1989), interagency relationships, like those found in the Tri-Party Agreement, rely upon workable levels of cooperation between the agencies involved to be successful. Ultimately, cooperation will depend upon the acceptance of clearly defined roles for each agency in ground rules that establish the division of labor, authority, policy goals, and priorities. In the Tri-Party Agreement, ground rules were established by two federal laws. The Resource Conservation and Recovery Act (RCRA) of 1979 gives Ecology authority over the treatment, storage, and disposal of hazardous waste within the state of Washington, while CERCLA gives authority for the clean-up of past practices at federal facilities to the EPA. Thus, these two federal laws put Ecology and the EPA in an independent or authoritative role of regulator regarding Hanford and put the DOE in the dependent position of regulatee (Rabe, 1986).

Davis and Lester (1989) say that relationships with such clearly defined roles should ideally be "accompanied by improved cooperation between federal and state administrators." However, from the beginning, the DOE's resistance to cooperation and integration has been consistent. An environmental engineer in the EPA's Hanford Project Office in Richland, Washington, characterized the outside imposition of regulations upon the DOE as a "learning experience" for that agency which requires a major change from its operating history (Sherwood int., 1991). It is difficult for an agency that has operated, until recently, without outside interference or oversight to relinquish control over policy decisions or operating procedures that have always been its exclusive domain (Nord int., 1991).

In contrast to the DOE's behavior, Ecology openly embraced the integration process while standing firm against the DOE's resistant behavior. Ecology has long had a reputation for its "aggressive, trailblazing" policies and management style. Ecology also had prior experience with the implementation of integrated environmental regulatory policies and was not easily intimidated by the DOE's resistance to integration (Rabe, 1986). One such example is the Washington Environmental Coordination Procedures Act (ECPA) of 1973, which mandates Ecology to control and integrate permits for projects that would affect the state's land, air, or water resources.

Through the Tri-Party Agreement, Ecology has forced the DOE to recognize the regulatory authority of Washington State in the Hanford clean-up, an achievement the project manager for Ecology calls a "tremendous coup" (Nord int., 1991). Relations with the DOE prior to the signing of the agreement were "very, very testy" and communication was characterized by "a lot of saber rattling" (ibid.). In the two years since the agreement took effect, the state believes relations between the regulators and the DOE have improved slowly but steadily. Today, officials at both Ecology and the EPA generally threaten the DOE with legal action only when that agency becomes intractable concerning a required milestone and only as a last resort (ibid.). Through defined roles, the Tri-Party Agreement established a structure for interagency cooperation where none had existed before.

Citizen Participation

One of the goals of New Federalism is to encourage citizen participation in policy formation. Surveys indicate that citizens believe it is easier to influence policies of state agency personnel than those of their federal counterparts (Davis and Lester, 1989). This participation is to be accomplished through public hearings and personal contact as agency personnel are lobbied to support one position or another. Ecology has indicated that citizen-expressed policy preferences which coincide with Ecology's policy priorities have been adopted. The project manager at Ecology believes the adoption of such requests appears to stimulate public support and interest in the decisionmaking process, and that the favorable publicity created by these situations strengthens Ecology's position when negotiating milestones with the DOE. This strengthening occurs when citizens publicly pressure elected officials through the media to support Ecology's policy decisions. In such instances officials are more likely to support Ecology's position in an effort to maintain good relations with their constituents. However, citizen preferences contrary to, or in opposition of, Ecology's policy priorities have not been adopted. This lack of adoption indicates that citizen influence over policy decisions is limited to policy goals also favored by Ecology (Nord int., 1991).

Agency personnel report that continual pressure at public hearings brought concerns regarding ongoing waste disposal at Hanford to the attention of agreement negotiators. Citizen interest groups such as the Hanford Education Action League (HEAL) and Heart of America complained that continued waste dumping by agencies charged with clean-up responsibilities was unacceptable and demanded that current and future dumping practices be addressed in the agreement milestones. The EPA called the position a "compelling argument" that agency personnel at Ecology agreed with, resulting in the inclusion of costly studies to evaluate the impact of thirty-three effluent streams still operating at Hanford at the time the original agreement milestones were being negotiated. The studies led to the shutdown of a number of effluent streams, the tank storage of some effluent waste, and the continued evaluation of the remaining effluent streams (Sherwood int., 1991).

A second example of direct citizen participation is the current effort by several citizen groups to make land use planning an additional milestone in the agreement. By testifying at public hearings and lobbying agency personnel and congressional staff, citizens have convinced members of the Tri-Party Agreement to pursue land use designations in future milestone change negotiations. The issue of future land use designation can have a dramatic effect upon the clean-up and restoration process. Different land use goals will likely require different degrees of clean-up effort. For example, returning the land to a pristine condition that could support farming or human habitation would require a great deal more effort, time, technology, and money than a land use goal that would simply stop further contamination of the site and safely contain past damage. A decision regarding land use for Hanford has yet to be made, but the EPA expects that the agencies involved will draw "battle lines" over the issue, with Ecology pushing for maximum clean-up efforts within the state (including a rather ambitious land use goal) as the DOE pushes for a minimum effort and investment. The EPA plans on taking a moderate position on the issue and expects to be somewhere in the middle (Sherwood int., 1991). Through public participation, the Tri-Party Agreement has allowed citizens to become a part of the solution by influencing policy priorities and developing policy goals. However, this influence has been strictly limited to goals that have also been agreeable to Ecology.

Political Support

Another factor, according to Davis and Lester (1989), that may restrict state policymakers from successfully implementing environmental programs is political opposition from factions that may have competing interests within the state. This development was apparent after the shutdown of the N-Reactor at Hanford in 1988 when DOE employees, many of whom were state residents, were confronted with the prospect of unemployment. Local government representatives naturally reacted negatively to closure efforts and, in an attempt to save jobs, favored a $50 million plan by the DOE to refurbish the aging reactor in order to continue plutonium production at the site. After a complete understanding of the scope of the clean-up project and the level of long-term employment was made known, support for the retooling of the reactor was largely abandoned. The clean-up project at Hanford now employs more people than the facility did during peak years of production, and the crews are assured of steady work for the next thirty years. Today, support for the permanent closure, dismantling, and clean-up of the facility is widespread and faces little opposition (Nord int., 1991).

Credibility

Another factor found to influence Ecology's ability to implement the Tri-Party Agreement was credibility. The issue of credibility was not specifically identified by Davis and Lester as an influencing factor for institutional capacity. However, agency personnel at Ecology believe the ability of the public to directly participate in the policy formation of Hanford's clean-up has helped to establish the credibility of the project in the eyes of the public, and that a high level of public credibility corresponds to citizen participation and political support which can help when negotiating milestones. Nord (1991) also asserts that the DOE's lack of public credibility has, in turn, bolstered Ecology's negotiating strength even more. For this reason the issue of credibility was included in the case study examination.

The issue of credibility is particularly important since documentation of past DOE operations at Hanford and other weapons facilities has become public knowledge. Public awareness that the DOE's forerunner, the Atomic Energy Commission, used the local communities in radiation exposure experiments without their knowledge or consent has seriously damaged the DOE's credibility with the public.[1]

According to Nord, discussion at public meetings has convinced him that the general attitude of the public toward the DOE is one of distrust. The project manager also feels that Ecology and the EPA are generally seen as credible in the eyes of the public, and suggests that public support for Ecology is often triggered when it publicly criticizes the DOE regardless of the issue at hand. A recent survey, commissioned by Ecology, indicates that the level of public trust is significantly higher in Ecology than in either the EPA or the DOE (Melevin, 1991). Even the DOE admits that lack of credibility is an ongoing problem that can only be remedied by future honesty and public participation in the process (Duffy int., 1991).

Another problem that is related to the issue of credibility is the length of time needed to complete the project. The scope of the problem at Hanford is so large, and the clean-up program so long term, that measurable accomplishments will be incremental and slow in coming. This kind of plodding progress rarely inspires public faith or political support. In addition, with the technical and financial challenges at hand, the thirty-year schedule for completion of the clean-up is likely to be optimistic. Therefore, it is critical that the dominant agency in the agreement be one that will maintain public confidence over the years (Sherwood int., 1991).

The need for long-term implementation of a policy program is not unique to Hanford and is, in fact, common when dealing with environmental problems. Other examples of long-term policy problems include forest management, acid rain, and other toxic waste clean-up. Because many environmental problems require long-term solutions, the credibility of the agency entrusted with implementing the solution may be as important as the other factors identified by Davis and Lester.

CONCLUSION

The Tri-Party Agreement reveals that Ecology's response to policy problems at Hanford has followed the model of interdependency provided by Davis and Lester. First, the agency was found to be highly dependent upon federal funds for the implementation of the clean-up program. However, instead of suffering from federal budget cuts, as Davis and Lester found is common when dependency is high, the Tri-Party Agreement succeeded in maintaining long-term access to those funds, thus ensuring the program's future. Second, Ecology was also found to have developed a high degree of institutional capacity. The ability to respond to increased administrative needs was evidenced by the agency's expansion in the 1980s. In addition, successful integration was accomplished without jeopardizing accountability or access to adequate staffing and technical resources. The importance of agency credibility was also made apparent as the state of Washington pursues solutions to the past operating sins of the DOE. Moreover, there are indications that credibility may be an influencing factor on political and public support for all long-term environmental policy programs.

Although certain factors may vary (such as the scope of the problem, the state's institutional capacity, or the immediacy of health risk from contamination) in similar situations, the lessons of Hanford are clear. Policymakers should consider the particular problems associated with poor credibility when developing and implementing programs where DOE participation is necessary, and especially when it is central. This case study indicates that public support for nuclear waste programs will be higher if state or local agencies have independent authority over the DOE. This has specific implications for nuclear waste projects currently under way across the country and their likelihood for long-term success. This study also provides an example of how states may successfully negotiate with the DOE and achieve an independent and authoritative role, in spite of any state's likely dependence on certain federal resources.

In general, the agreement has incorporated the best of federalism and a state-dominated system while avoiding the common pitfalls of both. It stands as an example of an interagency integration that is successfully implementing a long-term, complex environmental policy program.

NOTE

1. The 1949 experiment, known as the "Green Run," released 5,500 curies of iodine 131 into the atmosphere surrounding Hanford. According to DOE documents, the purpose of the experiment was to determine what kind of damage would be incurred after a nuclear attack where similar amounts of radiation contamination were encountered. Intentional and accidental releases of iodine 131 from 1944 to 1955 totaled 537,000 curies (Steele, 1991).

REFERENCES

Barilleaux, Ryan J. 1988. *The Post-Modern Presidency*. New York: Praeger.

Davis, Charles E. and James P. Lester, eds. 1989. Federalism and Environmental Policy. In *Environmental Politics and Policy: Theories and Evidence*. Durham, NC: Duke University Press.

——. 1987. Decentralizing Federal Environmental Policy: A Research Note. *The Western Political Science Quarterly*, 40, 3:555–565.

Gittell, Marilyn, ed. 1986. *State Politics and the New Federalism: Readings and Commentary*. New York: Longman Inc.

Melevin, Paul T. 1991. *Opinions on Hanford and the Tri-Party Agreement: Clean-up, A Telephone Survey*. Pullman: Washington State University.

Rabe, Barry G. 1986. *Fragmentation and Integration in State Environmental Management*. Washington DC: The Conservation Foundation.

Steele, Karen. 1991. Ground water effect "very serious." *The Oregonian*, March 10, pp. A1, A10.

Wald, Mathew L. 1991. Nuclear waste dumped into ground at Hanford. *The Oregonian*, March 10, pp. A1, A18.

Interviews with:

Leo Duffy, Assistant Secretary of Energy, September 9, 1991.

Timothy Nord, Project Manager for the Washington Department of Ecology, Hanford Section, September 9, 1991; November 23, 1991.

Doug Sherwood, Environmental Engineer for the U.S. Environmental Protection Agency in the Hanford Project Office, November 20, 1991.

Index

Editors and Contributors

J. HOLMES ARMSTEAD, Jr., is Associate Professor in the Department of Political Science at the University of Nevada, Reno. He has previously been on the staff at RAND and on the law faculty at Southern University.

BRUCE B. CLARY is a Professor in the Public Policy and Management Program at the University of Southern Maine. He has published widely on topics of environmental politics and policy.

BRIAN COOK is Associate Professor of Government at Clark University. He is author of *Bureaucratic Politics and Regulatory Reform*, and articles on environmental policy and public management.

TIMOTHY C. EVANSON is a doctoral student in the Department of Political Science at The American University.

MARCY JEAN EVEREST is a doctoral student in the Department of Political Science at the University of Oregon.

LEONARD S. GOODMAN is an attorney in Washington, D.C. He is a long-time consultant on transportation issues concerning nuclear and hazardous waste. His work has appeared in a variety of journals and law reviews.

ERIC B. HERZIK is Associate Professor and Chairman of the Department of Political Science at the University of Nevada, Reno. He has published in a number of journals on aspects of state politics and policymaking. His most recent book was *Gubernatorial Leadership and State Policy* (Green-wood, 1991).

MARIANNE LÖWGREN is Assistant Professor in the Department of Water and Environmental Studies at Linköping University, Sweden.

AMY SNYDER McCABE is Assistant Professor in Public Administration at Pennsylvania State University. She was previously a research associate at the Vanderbilt Institute for Policy Studies.

MICHAEL V. McGINNIS is Assistant Professor of Political Science at the University of Oregon.

ALVIN H. MUSHKATEL is Professor in the School of Public Affairs and Director of the Office of Hazards Studies at Arizona State University. He has published widely on topics relating to emergency management and was recently named to a research committee of the National Academy of Sciences.

KARLEN J. REED is currently a district court judge clerk and finishing her MPA degree at the University of Nevada, Reno.

E. ROBERT STATHAM is a doctoral student in the Department of Political Science at the University of Nevada, Reno.

JAMES A. THURBER is Professor in the School of Public Affairs and Director of the Center for Congressional and Presidential Studies at The American University. He has published in a wide range of journals and his work on nuclear waste policy has been previously sponsored by the National Academy of Public Administration.

Policy Studies Organization publications issued with
Greenwood Press/Quorum Books

Health Insurance and Public Policy: Risk, Allocation, and Equity
Miriam K. Mills and Robert H. Blank, editors

Public Authorities and Public Policy: The Business of Government
Jerry Mitchell, editor

Technology and U.S. Competitiveness: An Institutional Focus
W. Henry Lambright and Dianne Rahm, editors

Using Theory to Improve Program and Policy Evaluations
Huey-tysh Chen and Peter H. Rossi, editors

Comparative Judicial Review and Public Policy
Donald W. Jackson and C. Neal Tate, editors

Moving the Earth: Cooperative Federalism and Implementation of the
Surface Mining Act
Uday Desai, editor

Professional Developments in Policy Studies
Stuart Nagel

International Agricultural Trade and Market Development in the 1990s
John W. Helmuth and Don F. Hadwiger, editors

Comparative Studies of Local Economic Development: Problems in Policy
Implementation
Peter B. Meyer, editor

Ownership, Control, and the Future of Housing Policy
R. Allen Hays, editor

Public Administration in China
Miriam K. Mills and Stuart S. Nagel, editors

Public Policy in China
Stuart S. Nagel and Miriam K. Mills, editors

Minority Group Influence: Agenda Setting, Formulation, and Public Policy
Paula D. McClain, editor